What Teenagers Wish Their Parents Knew About Kids

Fritz Ridenour

What Teenagers Wish Their Parents Knew About Kids

WORD BOOKS
PUBLISHER
WACO, TEXAS

A DIVISION OF
WORD, INCORPORATED

WHAT TEENAGERS WISH THEIR PARENTS KNEW ABOUT KIDS

Library of Congress Cataloging in Publication Data
  Ridenour, Fritz.
    What teenagers wish their parents knew about kids.

    Includes bibliographical references.
    1. Parenting—United States. 2. Adolescence.
  3. Parent and child—United States.   4. Youth—United
  States—Attitudes. I. Title.
  HQ755.85.R53 1982   306.8'74'0973   82–50516
  ISBN 0–8499–0308–4

Scripture quotations in this publication are from the following sources:
  The King James Version of the Bible (KJV).
  The New International Version of the Bible (NIV), published by the Zondervan Corporation, copyright © 1978 by the New International Bible Society.
  The New Testament: A Translation in the Language of the People, (Williams), by Charles B. Williams. Copyright © 1937 by Bruce Humphries, Inc. Copyright © renewed 1965 by Edith S. Williams.
  The Amplified Bible (Amplified), copyright © 1965 by Zondervan Publishing House.
  The New Testament in Modern English (Phillips), copyright © 1958, 1960, 1972 by J. B. Phillips.
  The Living Bible, Paraphrased (TLB), copyright © 1971 by Tyndale House Publishers, Wheaton, Illinois.
  The New American Standard Bible, (NASB), copyright © 1960, 1962, 1963, 1968, 1971, 1972, 1973, 1975, by the Lockman Foundation.

TO KIMBERLY, JEFF, AND TODD
who kept their mom and dad on their toes, off
balance, and leaning on the Lord
and
to all parents who know something about
being in the same position

Contents

Acknowledgments

. . . To Jackie, super wife, super mom, better half.

. . . To Gary Hess, costruggler, teacher, friend.

. . . To Ernie Owen, who got the idea for this book and affirmed the author in the dark hours of the deadline.

. . . To David Lynn, young enough to be my son, old enough to be my teacher. Thanks for the insights.

. . . To all the "RA's," and other leaders of youth who arranged surveys and interviews with the young people quoted in this book. Thank you!

. . . To Arline Hampton, fastest and most willing typist in the West.

. . . To all the collegians, high schoolers, and junior high students who contributed to this book. In all cases I tried to honor your privacy and willingness to share your feelings. Some names were changed, where deemed necessary by the editors. Without you the book could not have been. Many, many thanks!!!

What? Another Book on Teenagers?

I'VE ASKED MYSELF this question almost daily since starting this book. With the incredible avalanche of family books on the market, why add another? Parenting books abound. If parents utilized a tenth of the information and inspiration available, many, if not most, families could prosper and blossom as never in history.

Let's Listen to the Kids for a Change

The answer to "Why this book?" lies partly in the title. A major part of my material comes from teenagers, most of whom were reared in Christian homes of various degrees of commitment. I have surveyed and talked with young people in junior high, high school, and college settings. I was particularly interested in responses from freshmen and sophomores in college, who have matured to some degree, but still vividly remember the struggles of junior high and high school years. Ironically, I found many 18- and 19-year-olds still struggling with the basic issues all teenagers seem to face.

I have asked them all to tell me what they wish their parents knew about what it's like to be caught in the land of limbo called "teenager." They are "big kids" now, but apparently not big enough for society (or their parents) to trust completely. And in another sense, they are not kids any longer. They see themselves as adults with all the drives, abilities, and ambitions that come with being a young adult. This is particularly true as they reach the last years of high school and first years of college.

For example, Cindy, 18, and a college freshman, said: "I am strong enough to handle the responsibility of being an adult. . . . They treat me as an adult, but I feel their fear that I may be hurt. I do not like to worry them and wish they believed in my strength more."

The first major goal of this book is to go to the teenagers and let them tell us what they see in parents: the faults and shortcomings, to be sure, but also the strengths and virtues. One of the pleasantly surprising parts of my research was learning that many young people are quite positive about their parents. They see room for improvement. They see our hang-ups and foibles. But for a goodly number, the so-called "generation gap" isn't a great gulf after all.

Denise, 18, a university sophomore, said: "As far as I can see, my parents and I have a relationship that is already rich and understanding. There are no generation-gap problems. My parents aren't really just parents, they are actually two of my best friends!"

At the high school level, Larry, 16, simply said, "I don't have to say anything; they understand."

And Nancy, 13 and a seventh grader, added, "There's really not much problem. My parents are great."

Of course, not everyone I talked to feels that positive. Some see a generation gap wider than the Grand Canyon. For a few it might as well be the Pacific Ocean. Some teenagers gaze wistfully across the gap wishing things could be better. A coed at a Christian college on the West Coast told me: "It would be great if my dad would just tell me, 'I love you.' I know that he does, but he has said it to me only once or twice in my whole life."

Other young people stare indignantly across the gap, asserting an independence they feel their parents are refusing to grant. A key question on my survey questionnaire asked: "If you could tell your parents one thing to help them understand and relate to you, what would you say?" Typical of many answers was one by a college freshman who said, "Don't try to raise me like you were raised. Take problems as they come and don't jump to conclusions. I'm not a child, and I'd like a chance to prove it" (Sandra, 18).

There were also many remarks about "getting on our level." An example is Mark, 16, who said, "They should move down a few levels and get on our (teenagers') level and try to realize what we are going through."

Edward, 18, added, "Parents should not be overstrict but try to be more on the kid's level. They should learn to trust a kid but be able to talk on their level and understand."

Three Major Needs Emerge

In conducting my survey I never intended to compete with the full-blown research projects that employ thousands of questionnaires, computers, and punch cards. Two excellent examples of this in the teenage field are Merton Strommen's *Five Cries of Youth,* a survey of 7000 church youth published in 1974, and the more recent report by Jane Norman and Myron Harris, *The Private Life of the American Teenager,* a massive study of over 160,000 junior and senior-high school students 13 to 18 years old.

Interestingly enough, the basic themes and problems that I found in surveying several hundred young people are the same ones that surfaced for Strommen or Norman and Harris. These refrains include:

1. A search for identity and self-esteem—to be respected as individuals and given "the chance to be me, not somebody else."

2. An almost desperate frustration over failure to communicate—"to be listened to, not just talked at."

3. A concern about parental use of authority and discipline—"to be trusted and treated like an adult, not a little kid."

Principles, Not Just Percentages

In pinpointing the three areas listed above I want to do more than give teenage quips and quotes mixed with provocative percentages. It is important to know what teenagers want us to know, but once we have their feedback, what do we do with it?

A second major goal in this book is to examine what teenagers are saying and draw out some practical principles and ideas for parenting. Many of my principles come from Scripture. The entire book, in fact, balances on Paul's instruction to parents in Ephesians 6:4: ". . . provoke not your children to wrath, but bring them up in the nurture and admonition of the Lord" (KJV). I believe Ephesians 6:4 contains a built-in tension that no parent can escape, particularly while he and his children grope through what the academics call "adolescence." Throughout the book I grapple with this mysterious tension, which is easy to see, but hard to solve.

In addition to scriptural principles, I want to share my survey of many fine parenting books currently available. My reading includes many Christian authors, as well as some non-Christian ones who are often valuable for their common sense, if not always their theology.

As a parent I have admired and profited from the work of Dr. James Dobson, Dr. Bruce Narramore, Norman Wright, Chuck Swindoll, Dr. Maurice Wagner, Tim and Bev LaHaye, and Ross Campbell, to name just a few who are well known in Christian circles. In addition, I have found much of value in the work of "secular" authors like Haim Ginott, Dorothy Briggs, Dr. Fitzhugh Dodson, and Dr. Thomas Gordon. While they do not write from a Christian or biblical perspective, many of their ideas can be used by the Christian parent *who builds on a solid Scriptural base*. Indeed, if Christian parents could learn to really use active listening and the "I" message, skills taught so feverently and skillfully by Ginott and Gordon, they would get along much better with their teenagers and carry out the instructions in Ephesians 6:4 much more effectively.

Plus a Few Personal Confessions

Although I include substantial discussion of useful skills and strategies, this is not your basic "how to parent" book. There are many excellent ones already on the market (see Appendix 2). My major concerns lie in two areas:

1. Attitudes
2. Relationships

After doing considerable research and rearing three children of my own to adulthood, I am convinced that attitudes are the key to building a solid relationship, particularly with a teenager. In fact, when life gets down to the nub, attitudes may be all you really have going for you.

A third goal for the book, then, is to compare my own experience as a parent with what my research reveals. Three key sources of input are my own children: Kimberly Currie, now 22, who made me a proud grandfather of Matthew Robert in August, 1981; Jeff, now 21 and a college sophomore; and Todd, now 18 and a college freshman.

I have gone to them and asked, "What do you wish I knew about you? What do you want to tell me about how I've done as your dad?" This was not easy. Lest you start to sniff a setup, let me assure you that my record as a parent is hardly spotless.

As youth editor for Gospel Light Publications in the late sixties and early seventies I wrote some nine books for use in teenage Sunday school classes. They were paperbacks, cleverly illustrated by the cartooning of Joyce Thimsen. They caught on, and I became something of a "youth expert." All this happened while my three children were still small. *Then* I had no trouble talking to other people's teenagers, in person or on paper. And meanwhile, my own kids were growing up. As I have told more than one audience, "I was a youth expert until my kids became youths."

They didn't grow up overnight, I know, but it still seems to have struck with an awful suddenness. The eager pleas to play, to go, to talk turned to gutteral sounds, "through-me" looks, and terse communiqués like: "Nothing." "Don't remember." Or "Can I have my allowance?" Not all the conversations were short. Some got lengthy as my teenagers bargained for loans to finance special projects or argued with the skill of Perry Mason to be allowed to stay out later than curfew as they traveled some incredible distance (to me) to visit "someone special."

For the past ten or eleven years I have groped in the foggy atmosphere familiar to most parents of teenagers. I've sought the fairest way to discipline, the most reasonable approach to unreasonable requests, the best way to grant allowances, use of the car, etc. I have also learned the prayerful way to wait "without anxiety" for the front door to shut softly, announcing that the last Ridenour eaglet has returned safely to the nest for the night.

I read Narramore's theories on logical consequences and found them not only logical, but attractive. I studied Dobson's exhortations on daring to discipline the strong-willed child and found new steel for my parental resolve to not be permissive. I marveled at the conversational wizardry of Ginott and Gordon and dedicated myself to active listening, "I" messages, total empathy, and unconditional positive regard. But alas, invoking Narramore's logical consequences often had unique consequences all its own. I dared to discipline but not always with the unruffled aplomb of one who is absolutely sure he is God's instrument of divine justice.

And what of those happy endings to the conversations between teenagers and fathers who use the wisdom of Gordon and Ginott? I am at a loss. Did Gordon and Ginott have kids like mine or did they just write some great dialog for fiction?

Ginott, for example, tells me how to make proper comments after my teenager does a less than satisfactory wash job on the car. I am not to question Todd's character, neatness or dedication to responsibility. Instead I am to say: "The car appears to need a little more work. When can you do it?"

According to Ginott's script, Todd is supposed to reply: "Why sure, Dad. I'll do it by tonight."

The problem, of course, is that Todd has another answer: "Looks good to me, Dad. No time left today. Got to run!"

Oh well, maybe the car looks okay after all. . . .

As I have fought the good fight, I haven't known any real Armageddons. It was more a matter of small skirmishes: not-quite-washed cars, not-quite-mowed laws, missed curfews, and unmade phone calls that could have saved my wife and me a lot of lost sleep. The list is long, and every parent has one. Indeed, you may be thinking: "I'd like to write a book. The title would be *What Parents Wish Teenagers Knew about Stress.*"

Every family knows about the skirmishes. They come with the territory. I've won my share, lost more than a few, and often wound up happy to settle for a tie. I give a play by play of several personal incidents in the hope you can learn from my mistakes, or at least empathize. I am guessing, too, that a lot of parents will read this book and say, "So he blew it there, too. They don't handle that problem very well either. I'm not the only one!"

A Semipro with Empathy

So I come not as the expert, the specialist, the spiritual giant who has stumbled only once or twice in his parenting career. I come as a parent who has been flattened more than a few times by the kids he was trying to love. I come as a father who has fallen on his face more than once as he slipped on banana peels that were his own doing.

I come as a husband who didn't always agree completely with his wife on "how to handle the children," but who always tried to reach a middle ground that met the needs of the situation. As a lot of parents know, the middle ground usually puts you right in the middle.

I come as a dad who loves his children very much, but isn't always sure of how to express that love in a way they think is "cool." I come admitting I don't handle rebuffs, silence, or inconsistency (theirs or mine) very well.

I also come as a reporter who finds it quite comfortable to go outside his family circle to talk with young people in high school and college-age groups and classes. I believe I can hear what they are saying as I sort out the honest pleas and wistful searching from the self-centered bravado and naïveté.

Finally, I come as a teacher committed to helping teenagers and parents apply the Bible where the rubber scorches the road more intensely than anywhere else—at home in that family circle where it can be cozy fun or a bear pit. Accordingly, I have constructed this book for multipurpose use. Moms and/or dads can read it alone or together and discuss the quizzes, insights, and issues. Or a Bible study group or class can study it as a course. I have taught many of the principles in this book to parents who have given me invaluable feedback and encouragement. (Actually, it's fairly easy to assemble a group of parents who have teenagers. They seem willing to cluster naturally together, much like a herd of moose being harrassed by wolves.)

I come as sort of a semipro with lots of empathy—for the parents and for the kids. I hope to be something of a bridge across Generation Gap, whether it's narrow or wide. At least I hope to help the generations meet somewhere on that bridge and maybe even sit down and talk. Granted, both sides need to do a lot of listening, as well as talking.

Maybe that's the whole problem: too many parents aren't listening because they're too busy telling their teenagers what they "need to hear." Too many teenagers aren't listening because— rightly or wrongly—they think they aren't being listened to, never have been listened to, and probably never will be listened to. With too many parents and teenagers we have all the makings, as Paul Tournier puts it, for a "dialogue of the deaf."

But it doesn't have to be so. Some simple secrets of success are there, waiting to be discovered. How well or often you use them is up to you. A lot—maybe everything—depends on your attitude.

What really works with teenagers? What do they want? What do they see as love, and what do they interpret as indifference or dictator tactics? On the following pages you can find out. From the mouths of babes grown tall come the clues to making Ephesians 6:4 more than a slogan.

He who has ears to hear, let him hear.

Unit I: Self-Esteem

Building Your Teenager's Self-Esteem—
While Trying to Keep Your Own

A major theme that filters through almost any conversation with teenagers is the need for self-esteem. Teenagers don't say in so many words, "I want high self-esteem," but they do talk a great deal about being individuals with thoughts, plans, and ideas of their own. They see themselves as persons with feelings, and they want to be treated like adults, "not little kids." In these first four chapters we will explore the foundational issue of self-esteem as we look at:

. . . the "generation gap"—is it really there?

. . . what do parents do that drives their teenagers a little crazy?

. . . why teenagers need encouragement so desperately.

. . . why teenagers feel they "don't get no respect."

. . . the vital question for parents who want to build their teenager's feelings of self-worth.

. . . the toughest job of all for parents of teenagers.

. . . how well do you know your teenager? Are you training him up in your way, or his?

. . . the key attitudes of understanding, respect, letting go, and acceptance.

19

1.

There Is a Bridge across Generation Gap

"It's hard to be a teenager . . . being a teenager now is harder than back then" **(Carl, 15).**

AFTER SERVING A substantial apprenticeship as father to three teenagers, I have often longed to talk with the apostle Paul. There are many things I want to discuss: the deeper meanings in Romans 7, what really happened in Corinth, but the first thing I think I'd want to chat about is a brief verse in the sixth chapter of Ephesians:

"And ye fathers, provoke not your children to wrath: but bring them up in the nurture and admonition of the Lord" (Eph. 6:4, KJV).

I've never had any trouble with the first three verses of the sixth chapter of Ephesians. Paul makes perfectly good sense when he says: "Children, obey your parents in the Lord: for this is right. Honor thy father and mother . . . that it may be well with thee . . ." (Eph. 6:1–3, KJV).

But that fourth verse has always intrigued me. In just seventeen words Paul creates a fine line so razor sharp that it's hard at times to find it, much less walk it. And it seems to me that somewhere in this verse is the key to the so-called gap between the generations. I have talked to teenagers and parents alike about the "gap." The first question I usually ask young people is "How wide is the *generation gap* between you and your parents? (a) A thousand miles? (b) A hundred miles? (c) Ten miles? (d) No gap at all?"

The answers vary. There are a few at either extreme: some feel

21

the gap is a thousand miles or more; others feel no gap at all. Most, however, list ten miles or maybe one hundred. For a lot of kids it seems to depend on the time of day (or night, if it's after curfew).

A key problem seems to be defining the term. *Generation gap* doesn't quite describe how teenagers—or their parents—feel. As I talk with all ages, I continually hear phrases containing the word *understand*. When I asked one group of college freshmen and sophomores to write down one thing they would like to say to their parents, any number of replies sounded like this:

"I have to grow, please *understand*" (Gail, 18).

"Just *understand* how it was for you when you were my age and please help me down on my level" (Kimberly, 18).

At another college one coed defined the generation gap as "the extent to which parents and their children *misunderstand* each other."

I've also asked Christian parents what they think of when they hear the words *generation gap*. One mother took most of the blame by saying, "Lack of *understanding* their (the teenagers') needs at their age."

A father in the group saw it both ways: "Sad—little or no communication. No desire to *understand*."

Lack of desire to understand seems to be at the heart of the problem. As St. Francis of Assisi put it: "Seek not to be understood, but to understand." Perhaps St. Francis took a cue from Paul's instructions in Ephesians 6:1–4. True, Paul tells the children to obey and honor their parents and he throws in a promise of long life in the bargain. The monkey seems to be on the back of the kids, but Paul doesn't even stop for breath before going on to say, "Fathers, (the Greek here can also mean "parents"[1]) provoke not your children to wrath. . . ."

How to Provoke a Teenager

What does Paul mean? The New International Version puts it: ". . . do not exasperate your children." The Amplified Bible uses the word *irritate*. Phillips Translation says: ". . . don't overcorrect your children. . . ." The Living Bible paraphrase is even more vivid: "Don't keep on scolding and nagging your children, making them angry and resentful."

Another clue is in a parallel passage in Colossians 3:21. Here Paul is giving similar advice to parents as he says, "Fathers, do not embitter your children, or they will become discouraged" (NIV). Commentators differ on whether or not Paul ever had children. Some believe he might have been married at a younger age, when he was a member of the Jewish Sanhedrin. Married or not, Paul realized that being a child (or a teenager) is not all fun and games. Teenagers do need understanding from parents, even if they can't always give their parents much understanding themselves. Paul knew it is all too easy to discourage and frustrate young people by making them feel that no matter what they do it isn't good enough.

As one high-school girl told me during a weekend retreat: "I try to do something nice for my mom, and instead of telling me I did a good job, she tells me the things I didn't do."

Parents can not only discourage children, they can also drive them a little bit crazy. As I conducted my surveys, another question I asked a lot of young people was: "How do parents make their teenagers resentful (drive them a little bit nuts)?" I offered three multiple-choice answers:

a. By talking too much or too long, repeating the same thing over and over.

b. By jumping to conclusions—assuming something is wrong, etc.

c. By not really listening to what their teenager is saying.

Curiously enough, the answer scoring highest in all groups that I surveyed, with an average of 47 percent, was the one on talking too much and repeating the same thing. Though I can't be sure, perhaps most of the students picked this answer as a way of saying their parents weren't really listening. When given the chance to tell their parents how they feel, young people often come up with comments like this:

"Please listen better and don't be so narrow-minded!" (Tammy, 18).

"Listen to my opinion; sometimes I am right" (Mary, 18).

"Listen to me, consider the difference in our ages, and try to see things through younger eyes sometimes" (Carole, 19).

Also scoring high on that same question, with 30 percent of the vote, was "jumping to conclusions." One college sophomore put it this way: "Please try to understand the things I do—don't reprimand me before listening to my side of the problem" (Pamela, 19).

"I Guess Moms Worry a Lot . . ."

When I talked with my own offspring about how Jackie and I did on jumping or not jumping to conclusions, we got mixed reviews. Jeff, our oldest son, looked back from age 21 and recalled that during high school, which was essentially a rebellious time for him, his mother and I were so conditioned to his breaking of rules that we would often jump to conclusions and assume he had done something wrong. "A lot of the time," he recalled, "I would think, 'Wrong or right, Mom and Dad will think I did wrong'—not all the time but it happened a lot."

Todd, our 18-year-old, can recall that his mother sometimes would jump to conclusions about what might be going on at a certain high school function he wanted to attend. "This irked me sometimes," he says, "because I steer clear of drinking and dope, but I guess moms worry a lot about their sons."

From Mom's side comes the recollection that she rode with Todd in his Toyota one day and the car reeked of smoke. Instead of even hinting that he might have been smoking, she simply asked, "Who did you give a ride to that smokes?" Not too surprisingly, Todd doesn't remember the incident, which might suggest that a lot of the generation gap is in the eye of the beholder.

Our daughter Kimberly, now 22 and a parent herself, breezed through high school with no problems regarding rules and responsibilities. She remembers being grateful that I "never jumped to conclusions,'' especially the day she spun out in our station wagon and called me to report that the car was up against the curb with the right wheel looking ''a little funny.''

Nurture Equals TLC

Jumping to conclusions, talking too much, continually criticizing—there are many ways to drive a teenager to distraction. Paul doesn't dwell on the problem in Ephesians 6:4; instead he goes right on to the solution: ''. . . bring them up in the nurture and admonition of the Lord.''

King James terms like ''nurture and admonition'' aren't too familiar to many parents today. They might prefer to call it TLC—tender loving care. The Greek word for ''nurture'' is *paideia*, which is also used in Scripture to refer to ''discipline,'' ''training,'' or ''education.''[2]

Most parents have heard a sermon somewhere or read a book that defined the word *discipline* not as ''punishment,'' but as ''positive training and teaching.'' The root meaning of the word is ''disciple.'' We've also heard sermons about discipling our children, leading them to Christ and helping them grow in the faith. Ultimately that's what Paul has in mind here in Ephesians 6:4 as he tells us to bring up our kids in the nurture and admonition ''of the Lord.''

''In the Lord'' is a key phrase for Christian parents. Children are to obey and respect us ''in the Lord.'' We are to discipline and train them ''in the Lord.'' One of my survey questions asked young people what they thought of how they were nurtured in the Lord. How did they remember their spiritual training and the kind of image of God projected by Mom and Dad? Typical of negative remarks were:

''They feel God is someone to fear most of the time. God is rarely discussed in our home'' (Sandra, 18).

''Sent me to church when I was small, but never discussed God with me directly'' (Jerry, 19).

"They preach at me too much and give me a picture of God as a very formal, unfun person" (Mark, 16).

Representative of the many *positive* remarks I got on the part parents played in the spiritual development of their children were:

"Taught us about the Lord and have shown me that God is loving, forgiving, understanding, and patient" (Elise, 17).

"They showed me the way to the church and to Christ" (Randy, 14).

"Presented a very healthy image of God to me—when I didn't want to go, she forced me and I'm happy she did" (Lori, 18).

The Family-Time Fiasco

It would be nice to be able to tell you that in the Ridenour household Christian nurture and discipling never missed a beat during teenage years. Alas, such was not the case.

We did a lot of nurturing of the kids when they were small— singing songs, reading Bible stories, and praying before bed— but as they got up toward junior high level, it got a little harder to hold their interest. They were big kids now and getting a little too old for "baby stuff."

Ironically enough, about the time Kim and Jeff hit junior high I had moved into a new position at Gospel Light Publications— Director of the Family Life Division and editor of a new magazine *Family Life Today*. With gusto, I threw myself into the task, which included the developing of Family Night ideas and programs to help parents bring up their children "in the nurture of the Lord." Naturally, I wanted to try some of these ideas with my own family and so I gathered my flock around me at dinner hour for a "blessed time" of devotions and Bible study.

My first mistake was trying to have family time before we ate. I was outvoted on that one, 4–1. Next we tried it after dinner, but problems arose here as well. At that time, all our children were "one-helping" types. They gobbled their food and were ready to leave the table before Jackie and I had finished the salad. Making them wait until we had finished eating was always a challenge;

allowing them to leave and finding them later was a greater challenge.

We eventually did get together, however, and I used all my consummate skill to make family time interesting and enjoyable. We did Bible reading, Bible memory verses, and Bible quizzes. We tried role plays, trust walks, and problem solving. We had a few good sessions, but, more often than not, we were victims of some strange force that caused friction and frustration.

Jeff, then about 13, was the catalyst. He had pulled down the "teenage curtain" around age 11 and, consciously or unconsciously (at 13, who knows?), he sought to sabotage the family-time gathering. And he succeeded. In a way, I played right into his hands, especially with activities like: "Let's all share a problem we might be having right now in our family." The idea was to uncover any possible areas of conflict. It did.

Jeff: "Kim always tries to boss me."

Kim: "Well, Jeff, you always do things you aren't supposed to while Mom and Dad are gone."

Todd: "Do you guys always have to argue?"

Mom: "Hey, let's make this a happy time. . . ."

Dad: "I agree. Let's try to be positive. How do you think we could all love one another more?"

Jeff: "Just get Kim off my back . . . she's always bossin' me. Heil, Hitler!"

Todd: "I'm leaving. . ."

Dad: "No, you're not. This is *family* time!"

Kim: "Jeff, you're so mean . . . (sob)"

Dad: "Okay, okay, I think we'd better pray. 'Dear Lord, please help us. . . .' "

I kept feeling guilty, not to mention embarrassed, about failing at family time. I had really wanted it to work and had always envied all those Mormon drivers with their smug bumper stickers proclaiming, "Happiness is family home evening." But I finally decided we might as well abandon family time. No one protested, in fact I think we all breathed a secret sigh of relief.

But I did not give up completely. For example, we still had

brief times of prayer while giving thanks at meals. I also tried to work individually with the children, but I still had trouble communicating at spiritual levels, especially with the boys. Perhaps the increasing tension with Jeff—it mounted steadily with his age—intimidated me. Maybe I just copped out. Whatever it was, I was not that effective.[3]

Jeff looks back on those years and gives his impressions: "One thing that bothered me when I was growing up, especially in junior high school, was my parents never discussed with me my relationship with the Lord, what I felt about God, who I thought He was, things like that. I would go to church every Sunday and I would learn verses and win Bibles, but I never had a relationship with my parents where I could talk freely about God.

"I know parents have this burning desire for their kids to be very Christian. I could tell there was pressure in my dad's voice when he talked about church, about obeying Christ, things like that. I read the pressure and I wished he could have just said, 'Hey, where are you at with God?'—with a little less pressure-type attitude."

As for family time, Jeff remembers that that was *my* idea, not his: "I felt forced to have devotions with the family. If I could have felt comfortable talking about God individually with Mom or Dad, it wouldn't have been a big problem doing it with the family. But the way it was, I really didn't want to talk about God in front of Kim and Todd."

Jeff pinpoints a basic problem that began for him while he was still in grade school. Jackie remembers he started defying authority as early as fifth grade. Without really realizing it, we lost communication with him and moved into the parent-trying-to-keep-child-in-line syndrome. By the time he hit junior high, Jeff was our family rebel and had retreated into his own stronghold of defiance.

With Jeff I learned there is a big difference between being a "youth expert" and being a parent of teenagers. Jeff called it "pressure in my voice" and I guess he was right. I thought I was being cool and relaxed, but he didn't read it that way. For all of

Jeff's teenage years I wrestled with guilt, depression, frustration, and anger as I tried to be a loving dad. I tried to "be cool." I tried to understand, but I usually wound up irritating and exasperating Jeff more often than having the warm father-son relationship I prayed for constantly.

But while I ached to communicate with Jeff, I enjoyed a painless relationship with Kim. She puts it this way: "I could always communicate with my dad because he would let me air my feelings and even let me cry. I never felt like I had to hold anything back because of what he would think. I just knew he accepted me for being me. When I was in high school, my mom and I sometimes clashed on little things, and Dad would always help me get the right attitude back without coming down hard on me. I could always tell him everything."

Don't Look for It, Build It

We started this chapter looking for a bridge across the generation (i.e. understanding) gap that seems to separate a lot of us from our kids to one degree or another. But after talking to hundreds of young people, and living with three of them for almost two decades, I believe you don't find this bridge, you build it by using Ephesians 6:4 as a blueprint.

Teenagers are asking for a few strokes of encouragement (". . . don't exasperate (and discourage) your children . . ."). Perhaps your kids are like mine. They can come on so strong and self-confident that there are days when I'd like to borrow a little self-esteem from *them*! But I've learned to look past the bravado and to see that their self-esteem is not as armor-plated as they let on. Some psychologists claim that many a child's self-esteem is in trouble by age 10 and in shambles by age 15.[4] It is a jungle out there. That's why they often come home with fangs bared or tail tucked between legs. As the teenager moves through the competitive, critical world of high school and college, he sees and hears plenty of reasons to feel unloved, unworthy, and incapable.

Jackie remembers how Kim, always on the thin side as a child and as a teenager, would come home from junior high and even high school to seclude herself in her room in tears. The reason was the terms of endearment used on her by schoolmates, male and female. One choice sample: "It's Skinny Bones Jones! Do you wear skis in the shower?"

Usually competent and confident, Kim couldn't handle the sting of ridicule and teasing about her lack of weight, especially her skinny legs. Sticks and stones didn't hurt her nearly as much as labels like "Petrified Toothpick," but giving her a few words of parental comfort wasn't easy. Fiercely proud, Kim hated to have us see her tears almost as much as she hated the teasing. She drew limited solace from Jackie's assurance that someday she would realize she was lucky to have slender legs. What helped most was that Mom "understood."

Almost all of us can list the things that used to get to us, especially going through high school. What teenagers don't need from parents is to be "irritated and exasperated to resentment" (see Eph. 6:4, Amplified Bible). Coping with schoolmates, not to mention coaches, teachers, and employers, has already taken care of that. Many of the young people I surveyed mentioned how they appreciated encouragement from parents. One college freshman put it eloquently when she said:

"Thanks for all your love, Mom and Dad, and I'm going to always need it. Your support and continual forgiveness have done more for me than you will ever know. I'm a very indecisive person and have often hurt you and others. Please continue to support me and let me know when I'm blowing it. I love you" (Julie, 18).

Teenagers also want direction (". . . bring them up in the training and instruction of the Lord"), and some of them are even willing to ask parents for it openly, as Julie's remark demonstrates. In many cases, however, they don't say much, they must watch how their parents live. A major theme running through many of the survey remarks was the *kind of example* parents set for their children. Those with a more critical eye reported:

High school junior: "They are both Christians and seldom show it as a good example" (Valerie, 17).

High school freshman: "My mom presented a good image of God and is happy I am attending youth group, but she is too lazy to drive me to church on Sunday morning" (Robyn, 16).

College freshman: "My father sent me to Sunday school but never went himself" (Karen, 19).

From the positive side, my survey also uncovered many young people whose parents modeled their faith consistently. Said a college sophomore: "My parents made only positive contributions to my spiritual development and have not pressed their own personal convictions on me but, rather, let me grow in Him with complete trust that I am safe in His hands."

College freshman: "They have taught me the way of the Lord and have shined their lights on me all of my life. They have never left the Lord. Their relationship to Christ is so very strong" (Victor, 19).

When I asked Todd what he thought of our example, he came up with one of his typically pithy observations. Yes, we were good examples, he said, except for some times when I got "pretty mad" at Jeff. "At least," he added, "you never cheated on your income tax."

Key Attitude #1: Understanding

Paul is saying a great deal in Ephesians 6:4, so much so that we'll be coming back to this verse again and again. What Paul may be saying loudest of all is that trying to *understand* your child is not just important, it is crucial.

I once asked a class of parents what is most important in child rearing? Skills, goals, or attitudes? The overwhelming answer was "attitudes," and I agree. Of course, parenting skills and goals are important. So are biblical standards. And when dealing with my children, correction and reproof are part of the game plan as I attempt to teach them responsibility, dependability, honesty, etc. etc. But I can push all this much too hard and much too far. And my attitude can easily come across as being more concerned with *my* standards and *my* values.

The result is that instead of hearing *love* and *understanding* they hear the clatter of brass and the clanging of cymbals.

Another thing Paul is saying in Ephesians 6:4 is the better I understand my relationship to God as my heavenly Father, the better I should understand and relate to my teenager. To paraphrase Paul, I'm not to provoke and frustrate my kids with disciplinary clumsiness or overkill. Instead, I am to rear them, teach them, guide them, and relate to them in the same way the Lord relates to me. It is hard to provoke or frustrate someone while you are showing them genuine understanding. Yes, I would like a little understanding, too, but if it comes to a standoff, the buck stops or starts with me, the parent.

There is little point in denying it. There has always been a gap between the generations and there always will be. Teenagers and adults are no more likely to see eye to eye than a giraffe and a dachshund. But they can try to understand each other. Parents often complain of lack of respect from teenagers and they turn the screws of responsibility a little tighter to try to get it. My son, Jeff, can tell you that doesn't work. So can a lot of other young people. What teenagers want is a little respect themselves. Feeling respected—"like a *real person*," as one high schooler put it—is something all young people want very badly. We'll look more at that in the next chapter, but before going on, try working through the questions below. How wide is the generation gap at your house? And how strong are you building your bridge of understanding to your teenager?

FOR THOUGHT, DISCUSSION, AND ACTION

1. This chapter gave various definitions of the "generation gap" by teenagers and parents. Without looking back, write your

definition. What do you think of when you hear the words, "generation gap"?

2. This chapter discusses Paul's phrase, "Provoke not your children to wrath." From the list below, choose several ways you might be provoking or discouraging your own teenagers. You may want to write in some additional ideas.

_____ Keep dwelling on   _____ Not listening
      problems   _____ Attacking teenagers'
_____ Continually complaining   culture, values
_____ No praise when it's   _____ Insisting things be done
      deserved   my way
_____ Too much control   _____ Prejudging before
_____ Constantly repeating,   knowing the whole story
      nagging, etc.   _____ Wanting things done
_____ Expecting too much   immediately

3. Now think of some ways to encourage your teenager. List at least three things you can do with your son or daughter that will make a real difference to him or her. Be specific.

4. Do you have any kind of family devotional times with your teenagers? If you are experiencing friction or other problems, could one explanation be that their feelings about God and faith are hard to discuss with the whole family? (See Appendix 2, "Resources for Parents," for additional sources of ideas on family time.)

5. One way to try to understand your teenager better is to use an exercise developed by David Lynn, a youth director in Tucson, Arizona. When David talks with parents' groups about their teenagers he gives them the following quiz to help them remember their own teenage years:

a. What is the first thought that comes to your mind when you think of being 16?

b. Describe your friends in high school.

c. Were you popular in high school? Why or why not?

d. If you could relive high school, what would you do the same/differently?

e. Describe your first love.

f. Describe what you had to do to be popular at your high school.

g. What fads were prevalent when you were in high school?

2.

But I Don't Get No Respect!

"I need a little more respect . . ." (Brad, 15).

WELL-KNOWN COMEDIAN Rodney Dangerfield has made a good living by pulling at his tie, rolling his eyes, and complaining, "I just don't get no respect!"

A lot of teenagers seem to know what he means. When I surveyed one group of college freshmen and sophomores on what they wish their parents knew about them I got many answers like this:

"Please try to understand the things I do. Don't reprimand me before listening to my side of the problem" (Pamela, 19).

"Be concerned and suggest things to me, but don't force me. Allow me to make my own decisions" (Hans, 18).

"I have to be myself. I can't be anyone else or act like anyone else. I just have to be me" (Kathy, 18).

At the high-school and junior-high levels the remarks ran about the same.

"When I get in trouble or get grounded, listen to my opinion and see why I don't think I did anything wrong. Don't get so hyper over report cards, and let me make some decisions on clothes and shoes. Don't make me dress so ridiculously" (Stacey, 15).

"Sometimes when I'm trying to tell my parents something, they'll cut me off and not let me finish" (Scott, 14).

Parents who walk into their rooms without knocking, or who "snoop" in their personal belongings, drew special fire.

Roxanne, 14, feels her parents don't respect her as a person when, "They walk into my room without knocking most of the time."

Michelle, 15, remembers: "I wrote a letter to one of my friends, and I found it lying on the bed. My dad had told me it was open but it wasn't open, and I know he had read it. It had a lot of personal stuff in it, which I really didn't want him to know. Then he got all mad at me and accused me of all this stuff . . . and everything."

Pam, 16, has an ongoing problem with her mother getting in her mail and her diary. She says, "She's read . . . she went through all my diary. I even caught her in the act one time, and I just stood there and said, 'Mom, what are you doing?' And I got so scared because I really wrote personal things in there. And she just goes invading my privacy and I just felt like she didn't trust me or she didn't have any respect for me. . . ."

Shades of Ephesians 6:4! Paul's words are especially potent in The Living Bible paraphrase: "And now a word to you parents. Don't keep on scolding and nagging your children, making them angry and resentful. Rather, bring them up with the loving discipline the Lord himself approves, with suggestions and godly advice."

The thread in what all these teenagers are saying could be put this way: "I don't want to be put down and frustrated. I know I'm supposed to respect my parents, but I'd like a little respect myself."

Is Respect Too Much to Ask?

Are young people asking too much? Are their complaints legitimate, or should they just button up and buckle down until they get out on their own? It all depends on your point of view. Dr. Ross Campbell, a psychiatrist and family counselor, believes that a primary problem in many families is that the parents have a distorted idea of what adolescence is and what to expect from their youngsters. While they truly love their teenagers, they don't know how to convey that love in a way that makes their kids feel loved and accepted.[1] Says Campbell in his excellent book, *How to Really Love Your Teenager:* ''As we work with teenagers who have problems, a common interweaving thread constantly presents itself as either the cause or the aggravator of their troubled situations—a feeling of not being loved or cared for by their parents.''[2]

Feeling loved and cared for is at the heart of good self-esteem and self-respect. If you listen between the lines, that's exactly what teenagers are asking for when they say: ''Please try to understand what I do . . . don't force me . . . I have to be myself . . . don't make me dress so ridiculously.''

Of course it's easy to respond to all this with a certain amount of adult impatience. After all, teenagers often have far more by way of clothes, money, possessions, food, entertainment, etc. than their parents ever did. They should be grateful. They shouldn't feel so put down and put out. They get too dramatic. They exaggerate. . . .

Perhaps, but feelings are funny. They don't operate according to logic or rational thinking. Feelings just *are*—and teenagers have a lot of them. One major reason they are so full of feelings and emotion is that—*contrary to their opinion—they are children, not adults*. Ross Campbell writes: ''Teenagers are children in transition. They are not young adults . . . a teenager may be bigger, smarter, stronger, or in other ways superior to his parents. But emotionally he is still a child. He continues to need to feel loved and accepted by his parents.''[3]

Campbell goes on to say that many people in authority over teenagers overlook their childlike needs for love and acceptance, for being taken care of, for knowing that someone really cares for them. Ironically, a lot of parents fall into this category of adults who don't seem to care, and often it's more by accident than design. It's just too easy to get preoccupied with keeping the bills paid or worrying about problems at work. This was the case with Kim, a 16-year-old high-school junior: ''My mom will come home from work and talk about all the problems. And she'll go on until it's time to watch TV or it's time to go to bed, and then she goes to bed . . . like she's in her own little world. And I'm not part of it.''

The generation (i.e. understanding) gap takes its toll. Parent and child seem to get cut off from each other. It's not deliberate on anyone's part. It just happens. Teenagers grow up feeling a certain lack—of love, of respect, of success. Call it what you will— something's missing. They become adults who struggle with lack of self-esteem and self-worth. And they have children who feel these same lacks, and the cycle continues.

Perhaps you are well aware of the cycle. You may even feel trapped in its tentacles yourself. Can parents who have less than high self-esteem break the cycle and reach out to help their teenagers, who may already be suffering from lack of self-worth? There are no pat answers, but there is a way to start. Just knowing the ingredients of self-esteem can be a major step toward a better understanding of yourself and your teenagers and why one or both of you is muttering, ''I don't get no respect.''

Just What Is "Self-Esteem"?

Self-esteem is, simply, how you feel about yourself, how much you like—or dislike—you. Dorothy Briggs, author of *Your Child's Self-Esteem,* ties it to two basic needs: (1) to be loved, and (2) to feel worthwhile.[4] Maurice Wagner, holder of doctorates in theology as well as psychology, believes that three major feelings integrate to form the essential elements of self-esteem:[5]

1. I belong.
2. I am worthwhile.
3. I am capable.

When we feel we belong, we feel wanted, accepted, cared for, and enjoyed.[6] Christian parents especially may feel they have always tried to make their children feel all those things and more, but the understanding gap that yawns during teenage years can still make a young person feel he isn't accepted.

A college freshman wrote on his questionnaire: ''Try to understand the seriousness of the things I believe. Accept me. I may look like a kid in your eyes, but in others' and my own I'm almost an adult (man). Let me fall on my face, so to speak, so that I can learn to walk on my own" (Bob, 19).

A freshman at another school put it much more briefly when he asked his parents "just to accept me" (Jim, 18).

And at the same school, a sophomore made this poignant plea: "Take me and love me as I am!" (Mary, 19).

When we feel worthy we feel, "I am good" or "I count" or "I am right." Feeling worthy means that we sense positive attitudes from others and their hearty endorsement of our actions.[7] Teenagers often feel less than hearty endorsement of their ideas and actions from parents as demonstrated by Beth, an 18-year-old college student who wrote: "Teenage years are very turbulent. We need to learn and figure things out on our own. Parents can give advice and direction, but they shouldn't spoon-feed their morals, beliefs, and standards to us. They need to respect us or shouldn't expect us to respect them."

At another college a freshman's questionnaire had a little advice for parents and a lot of praise: "Please understand that I'm changing and taking uncertain steps in life. I will make mistakes, but I will learn from them. I just need you to be there and support me. My parents are very supportive of my goal—college education plus graduate education. I think that, in general, kids have to see that their parents are people and parents must see that their kids are people just like themselves and they need each other to be the best of friends and each other's No. 1 fan! Thanks!" (Alice, 19).

My own son, Jeff, looked back on his rebellious high school years and remembered this bright spot:

"I don't think I ever told you this, but it was important for me to know you understood what I was doing and that you approved. Like even when I got out of high school and you said, 'Hey, that's neat that you got your new job.' That really was a big deal to me. And like my basketball ability . . . that was good. Sometimes you went overboard—those big signs when I came home—'Nice job, Mr. Clutch.' But that was neat when you did approve. It made me feel good."

When we feel capable, we feel adequate and strong. As Maurice Wagner puts it: "It is the 'I can' feeling of being able to face life and cope with its complexities."[8] Wagner goes on to say that feelings of competence begin in preteen years and develop during teenage years. Not surprisingly, success builds feelings of competence; failure does not.[9]

As I surveyed college and high school students alike, I heard different messages regarding their feelings of competence. A large number come on strong with the typical, "C'mon, folks, I'm a big kid now" routine. For example: "I am growing up and you have to learn that I would like my chance to be independent. I don't think it is right to say no to things because you want to protect me from the 'bad world out there' " (Lisa, 19).

Other young people feel confident but are still looking for a little help from home. A high school junior said: "I am a teenager and I need to succeed as well as fail and I need to become more independent. They can help me by giving me confidence to go out and get a job and save my money on my own." And then she added, "I love ya. I hope you can experience the love from the Lord as I have" (Jennifer, 15).

One college sophomore was quite open about feeling less than adequate and wanting her parents' help. As she described how her parents could have helped her more during earlier teenage years she said: "I needed more encouragement and praise. I needed more time and fellowship through activities and more frequent conversations. I'm a sensitive girl, understanding and sincere. I'd like to talk to my mom more openly about my boyfriend, especially how to handle sexual desires so I can stay in keeping with God's Word. She doesn't have time for me. Or, when she does, I feel like she's not really understanding. I'm embarrassed to talk openly to her because I feel like she won't approve or accept my feelings. So, I feel like I always have to be my best. It doesn't give me any room to deal with my humanness and faults and know that I'm loved" (Denise, 19).

To feel loved as we try "to deal with our faults and humanness" is not a bad commentary on what self-esteem means to each of us.

To feel we belong is critical, and for the child, that always starts (or stops) at home. As we feel loved and accepted we feel worthy. We are able to accept ourselves. And, knowing we belong and are worthy helps us feel capable—able to cope with life. We may fail from time to time, but if we have enough feelings of worthiness and belongingness, we can bounce back and try again.[10]

Building Self-Esteem in Your Teenager

What, specifically, can you, the parent, do to build self-esteem in your teenager? As I have worked with parent classes and discussion groups, several practical principles for building a good self-concept in children have emerged. In the rest of this chapter we'll look at some ideas for building feelings of *belongingness* and *worthiness*. In chapter 3 we'll zero in on helping your teenager feel *capable*.

How well we do with building our teenager's feelings of self-worth revolves around a vital question:

Do my parental goals and priorities foster the building of high self-esteem in my child, or are my real goals and priorities centered somewhere else?

In one class of parents I taught for several weeks, one of the assignments was to rate ten parental goals in order of importance (from 1, for most important, to 10, least important). The goals are listed below, in the order the class rated them. If you are anything like the parents in my class, putting some of the choices ahead of others will be difficult, if not impossible. But try it anyway, according to your own parental priorities.

1. Rearing children who know God through Christ.
2. Rearing children who are confident, with good self-esteem.
3. Rearing children who are open and honest.
4. Having time for each child.
5. Rearing children who are obedient and respect their parents.

6. Rearing children who are responsible and good decision-makers.
7. Rearing children who are well behaved, a credit to the family.
8. Rearing children who are well dressed and groomed.
9. Having a clean home, especially the bedrooms.
10. Rearing children who like the same magazines, TV shows, and music as you do.

How did you match up with the above group? Obviously any class of Christian parents (as these people were) would rate "Rearing children who know God through Christ" as the No. 1 goal. After that they listed goals that center on building confidence and self-esteem as well as openness, honesty, responsibility, and decision-making skills. Not as high on their list were things like a clean house, or well-groomed children who like the same TV and music as Mom and Dad. I congratulated the class on their insight. They put their adult values second to things that would build and nurture their children. And then we grappled with just how well we were trying to achieve these noble goals.

A clue to achieving all of these goals is one of the goals itself. The group had rated this particular goal as No. 4—Having time for each child. We talked about how this just might be the most important thing a parent could do to build good self-esteem in his children. No matter how much a parent may say, "I love you" with words or gifts, there is no substitute for your time—for putting your minutes and hours where your mouth and pocketbook can't possibly go.

We'll Get Together, Son—Sometime

If you're like me you have probably heard sermons or read books about how crucial it is to give your children quality time. In one group I interviewed at a strongly conservative Christian college, a few of the students turned out to be in their early twenties.

They remembered teenage years vividly, however, and several were particularly bitter about the lack of time their fathers had had for them when they were younger. A prime example was Tim, a 22-year-old junior, who felt his parents tried "to show their love with things, not with time and caring."

Tim recalls that his family owned their own company and while his dad didn't travel a lot, he was still always working. "I would be around the plant, but he didn't spend a lot of time personally with me talking, and when I started to play, or go out to play catch, he was always too tired. I feel I have never gotten to know my father, the things he has done in life, the mistakes he has made."

Tim added that he grew up hating his father. He went into sports, but his dad was never around to see him play. He says sports were his source of self-esteem, but "I stayed to myself mentally and never let my parents know what I was thinking."

In the same group Mike, 23, related a similar experience and observed: "I think with kids growing up, a big thing is time, quality time with parents, not just, 'Let's do this' and do it and it's over."

Mike believes parents should differentiate between "doing things for the event, or doing things for the person. Make the central point the person, not the event. For example, I would rather my parents would say, 'Let's talk,' instead of 'Let's go to the movies.' "

Dan, 22, agreed with Mike, but, in his case, he could look back on one particularly happy time when he and his father spent a couple of days driving together in a car. Dan was in high school at the time and remembered: "He told me a lot of stories about things he did in high school, and I could really relate to what he went through because it was like things I went through. I saw my father from a wholly different perspective."

One other member of the group of 20-year-olds was Steve who also recalled quality times spent with his parents. He remembered: "My parents were both teachers, and we would spend a lot of time traveling in the summer. We'd go out and explore things, like the

Grand Canyon. And that gives you self-worth because you can sit back in the family and talk about what you learned and what you saw. That was really meaningful to me.''

Real Priorities—the Bottom Line

Priorities—one way or another you can hear their importance in what all four of these students are saying. I can have many excellent parental goals, but my *real* priorities—how I actually spend my time—reveal the bottom line every time.

Frankly, it's much easier to control the time situation when your children are small. If you still have younger children coming up, you may want to go over your *real* priorities to see just how much time you actually spend with them. If you have teenagers, you may find, as I have, that spending time with them can be a real problem. In fact, *finding* them can be a real problem.

You don't really schedule a teenager, you sort of wing it according to the moment—his moment. A good example is my 18-year-old son, Todd. I've been working on this chapter during Easter vacation week. Todd has been home most of the time, not by choice, but by doctor's orders. He has that strange malady that often hits teenagers: mononucleosis. For the past three days he has operated with the same routine: incommunicado before noon (with or without mono Todd is allergic to morning) and perking up a little after lunch. Each afternoon for the past few days, he has dropped into my den for a chat unannounced and without an appointment.

I am so far behind on the deadline for this book I am in danger of being lapped, but I still stop to talk about his latest plans for rebuilding his 1953 pickup or turning our garage into a woodworking shop. I don't make this "sacrifice" because I'm the noble perfect parent. In fact, at this stage of the parenting game it's no sacrifice at all. To be honest, I like talking with Todd, and besides, his truck is in pieces all over my garage, which he plans to convert into an area full of very expensive woodworking machinery. With all this going on, it is always good to keep communication lines open, deadline or no deadline.

When all three of our kids were small, I got into the familiar routine of the Christian layman: working long hours on my job and spending even more long hours in church ministry. Fortunately I came to my senses in a Christmas Eve church service while my oldest child, Kimberly, was still in grade school. Since then I have always tried to spend time with all three children.

Kim and I are good pals, but I suppose the two boys still got the best of it. For example, from third to eighth grades I coached them in a Little League type of basketball program. Kim reminds me, however, that I spent quite a bit of time helping her with sports like softball and basketball. I'm glad I took the time to do everything I could. In fact, I wish I could have done more. As Kim, Jeff, and Todd hit high school, their time became more and more their own. Eventually I had to make appointments with *them.* So I learned to persevere. Now I grab the moments for "just talking" when they come.

Key Attitude #2: Respect

In chapter 1 we started talking about the importance of attitudes by discussing the need for "understanding." You can have all kinds of standards and goals, but attitudes are what make it all fly—or crash. Obviously the key attitude being pushed in this chapter is *respect,* and the countless ways it can be shown.

Our daughter, Kimberly, remembers an incident I had totally forgotten. My 89-year-old father was dying of kidney failure. He was on oxygen, in a coma, and I wanted to take all three children to see him one last time. Kim, then 14, did not want to go. She cringed at the thought of seeing Grandpa with tubes and oxygen paraphernalia. At first I tried to insist she go, but as we talked I could see Kim was really uncomfortable with the prospect, and I finally excused her. She could remember Grandpa as she had last seen him, when he talked and laughed with her. "That really showed me you understood and respected my feelings," Kim told me later.

In summing up the key attitudes in chapters 1 and 2, we find more guidelines for making Ephesian 6:4 a practical reality:

Provoke not your teenagers to wrath.
Instead:
Try to understand them and show them a little respect
by making them feel they belong and that they are worthwhile.

It can and does happen. Some students I surveyed said of their parents:

"I love them and the last thing I want to do is deceive them, because I respect them more than anyone in the world" (Kathryn, 18).

"I am grateful for your being interested and caring enough to bring me up in the church with a constant care for me and what I'm doing" (Sue, 18).

It doesn't take tremendous insight to see that the parents of these two students have done a fine job of making their daughters feel that they belong and are worthwhile. In chapter 3 we will add the third leg to the stool of self-esteem—feelings of competence. First, however, try using the suggestions below to measure your own self-concept and to take inventory on specific things you are doing to build a good self-image in your teenager.

FOR THOUGHT, DISCUSSION, AND ACTION

1. It's not too hard to think of ways we want our kids to show us respect: speaking softly, being obedient and mannerly, doing things when asked, etc. Surely, this isn't too much for a parent to ask. But what about putting the shoe on the other foot? What specifically can you do to communicate respect to your teenager? Following are a few suggestions; you can add others.

a. Listen—really listen—to what they are saying (see chapter 5).
b. Admit when you are wrong and they are right.
c. Grant their right of privacy (room, mail, etc.).
d. Treat them more like adults than children (especially in front of peers).

2. As you analyze your own self-esteem, in which areas do you feel strongest? Where do you feel weak or in need? Rate yourself from 1 to 10 (10 being high) on the following:

_____ I belong (feel I'm loved, accepted, cared for, enjoyed).
_____ I am worthwhile (feel I count, do things right, have good self-respect).
_____ I am capable (feel adequate and strong, I can cope and handle things).

3. For the Christian, self-esteem (perhaps a better biblical term is *self-acceptance*) begins with God. People—even our loved ones—may fail to give us the support we need (sometimes they aren't capable of giving just the support we need; on other occasions they aren't really aware of our needs). God's love, however, is constant. Remember that:

. . . you belong to God because you can always say with Paul, "I am persuaded, that neither death, nor life . . . nor things present, nor things to come . . . shall be able to separate us from the love of God, which is in Christ Jesus our Lord" (Rom. 8:38–39, KJV).

. . . God makes you feel worthy because you know that you are ". . . found in him, not having a righteousness of my own that comes from the law, but that which is through faith in Christ—the righteousness that comes from God and is by faith" (Phil. 3:9, NIV).

. . . God is the source of your competence and you can know this by always remembering, "I can do all things through Christ which strengtheneth me" (Phil. 4:13, KJV).

The above verses aren't some magical little formula that you can repeat once a day and come out with great self-esteem. But what these verses do point to is the very bedrock for self-esteem—a solid relationship with God through Christ. This is where you must start.

4. Here are some additional ideas for building a good self-image:

   a. Read some good books on self-esteem. Excellent efforts by Christian authors include: *The Sensation of Being Somebody,* by Maurice Wagner (Zondervan); *You're Somebody Special,* by Bruce Narramore (Zondervan); *Hide or Seek,* by James Dobson (Revell).

   b. Of course, support from others never hurts. If possible, talk with your spouse or a friend about how you feel. Who knows? You may get a mutual self-esteem-builders society going.

   c. Do everything you can to build self-esteem in others: your spouse, your children, friends, and neighbors. Making others feel appreciated and worthwhile can make you feel that way too. And who knows, those others may return the favor.

   d. If your self-esteem is really in shambles, you need special care. Don't be too proud to talk to your pastor, a counselor, or a psychologist.

5. Decide on some specific things you will concentrate on this month—and in coming months—to build your teenager's self-esteem. You already made a good start by thinking of ways to show them respect (see 1 above), but here are some other ideas:

   a. Be generous with the compliments, but be sure you are sincere and on target. Teenagers can smell a phony compliment every time. Sometimes on the surface they aren't too receptive to well-deserved praise, but keep coming at them. Underneath they appreciate it.

   b. Value your teenager's ideas. They may differ from yours, but valuing is different than agreeing. Sometimes the teenager can be ''off the wall,'' on other occasions he is ''right on.'' Make it safe for him to be in either position.

c. Be sensitive to your teenager's emotions. He is a walking volcano of feelings and can erupt at any time, particularly when he is embarrassed.

d. Try to avoid sending your teenagers on guilt trips. They need "space" and they need to separate from you as they develop independence. Avoid remarks like, "You're never home, don't you care about us?" and "You need to think about someone besides yourself, young lady." The truth is, teenagers *are* thinking a lot about themselves. They need help sorting it all out.

e. Be patient—with their impatience, their tendency to label you old fashioned, out-of-date, ancient, etc. It is amazing how modern you will become in a few years—if you last.

3.

Deparenting—
Your Toughest Job

"I am growing up . . . I would like my chance to be independent"
(Lisa, 19).

WE HAVE LOOKED at two important legs of the stool of self-esteem that has to support each of us all our lives:

Belongingness—"I'm loved and accepted by others."

Worthiness—"I have value and can accept myself."

In this chapter we zero in on that critical third leg of the self-esteem stool, which in some ways, might be the most important of all to the teenager:

Competence—"I am capable. I can do it."

Competence is that feeling that enables us to cope, that we can handle whatever life throws at us: deadlines, responsibilities, problems. One of the most encouraging statistics in my survey of teenagers came from their answer to the question: "My parents have confidence in my ability (a) always, (b) sometimes, (c) seldom."

Sixty-five percent of the respondents answered "always" and another 32 percent said "sometimes." Only 3 percent checked "seldom." As I talked with students, I often heard them say that their parents were behind them, or that they were supportive. Some said their parents offered encouragement in words like, "I know you can do it."

That's a good start in building feelings of competence. Everyone likes to hear words of encouragement, but it's also nice to see those words backed up with actions. It is right here that parents seem to stumble. Paradoxically, parents may say "You can do it" to their children, but there seems to be a sharp difference of opinion of what "it" is. In practically every interview or conversation I had with teenagers, I heard the complaint that is exemplified in a remark by 15-year-old Brad who said: "I am old enough to make important decisions and my judgment is good enough."

Said one college freshman: "My parents tend to be too concerned with 'how things look.' They trust my judgment but are worried about what other people would think—even if no one would ever know the situation. I would like them to give me more freedom to make those 'gray area' decisions" (Margy, 18).

A sophomore at the same school had this to say: "I do what I do because I choose to do it. I respect your opinions although I do not agree with you all the time. You have given me wisdom to make my own choices, and I have done so on many occasions" (Erik, 19).

A high school junior living on the East Coast made this eloquent plea: "I realize you have probably undergone all the situations I now face, and know much better than me what will be the outcome according to what decisions I choose and what paths I decide to take. And I know you are only trying to show me the best outcome when you try and decide a situation for me, but please, I want to decide for myself. I want the freedom to decide what to do on my own, right or wrong. And no matter what the outcome, I will be happy because I decided for myself. Sometimes I resent your trying to run my life. Please, if you love me, give me more freedom" (Todd, 17).

Another high schooler put it more briefly and said: "I am 15 and really can take care of myself sometimes (not to be sarcastic)" (Kelly, 15). And a junior high student added: "Let me try things out. Let me know what it's like and let me decide" (Julie, 14).

How to Work Yourself Out of a Job

The above are just a few samples of dozens of similar comments. It seems to be a stand-off. Teenagers are saying, "We can handle things,'' and parents are replying, ''No you can't . . . you're not quite ready, you may ruin your life, etc. etc.'' To put it in biblical terms, many parents are trying to train up their children in the way they should go and the children are saying, ''Okay, we're ready, let us go!''

Who is right? To some extent, both sides have a point, but the parents come off the bad guys because they are grappling with perhaps the most difficult task they have: learning the fine art of *deparenting*.

And what is deparenting? While most of us have had moments when we would like to *de*-parent by ''sending *de* child to *de* moon with *de* one-way ticket,'' that's not what the word means. To deparent is to work yourself out of the job of totally caring for your children and being completely responsible for them. To deparent is not to become a nonparent. We are always parents to our children. But as they grow up, we become less their controllers, more their guides, and finally their friends on equal terms.

It sounds simple, but it is not. No area is more sensitive for the parent of teenagers than learning to deparent at the right rate of speed. Parents know instinctively that if they go too fast, they can lose the child completely. An absurd illustration would be allowing a three-year-old to play along the edge of a busy freeway. Trouble is, children don't stay three years old. They start *driving* on freeways. Deparent too slowly and you usually frustrate the child—particularly the teenager. The result is that you both go a little bonkers with continual arguments and hassles.

We seem to be back to square one. Teenagers think they can handle about anything. Parents ''know'' they can't. What we need is a *plan for deparenting*.

To put it in teenage parlance, I'm not sure if you are ''into'' charts, but the one on page 53 is not a bad way to picture the challenge and goal of parenthood and deparenting. It was developed by my good friend, Gary J. Hess, Coordinator of the Secondary Guidance and Attendance Division of the Glendale (California) Unified School District. Gary is also an instructor in a Master's Program at the University of LaVerne (California) where he specializes in instructing public school teachers in resolving conflicts and developing communication skills. He also currently teaches in an adult elective program in his church. Over twenty-five years of teaching and working with youth, plus rearing two daughters, all go into Gary's Plan for Deparenting. Here's how it works.

At birth, and when the child is very young, the parent has total responsibility for the child's behavior and well-being (the area called "Parents' Domain of Responsibility"). Very early in the child's life, however, there are areas where you start to "negotiate responsibility." As you see your child becoming capable of certain tasks you turn that responsibility over to him. The goal is that eventually—ideally sometime between 18 and 21—the child is completely responsible for his own behavior. Then everything, as the chart says, will be in the "Child's Domain of Responsibility."

The Plan for Deparenting chart is a picture of how you hope to see your child "grow up." As you deparent, more and more responsibility falls upon the child and less and less upon you. By age 21 (you hope) the child is a fully functioning adult. In a real sense, of course, you are still the parent and always will be, but now you are more the friend than the authority figure.

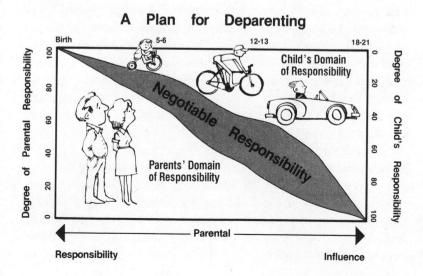

Sadly enough, many children grow to adulthood and become quite responsible, *but their parents never fully deparent.* The grown child always feels like he is being bossed, controlled, or manipulated. Many a grown adult always feels "like a little kid" when around his father, mother, or both. The plot of the Academy-Award-winning film, *On Golden Pond,* is partially built on this kind of relationship between the aging father (played by Henry Fonda) and his mid-forties daughter (played by Henry's real daughter, Jane Fonda).

According to the chart, however, the way to avoid making your child feel like the perennial "little kid" is to start negotiating responsibility when he is very young. An infant can't take much responsibility at first, but it doesn't take long for him to start. Toilet training is an earthy example of how child and parent negotiate and eventually the child winds up "in charge" of this part of his life (with luck, before Mom or Dad winds up a basket case).

Right here, please note a key point: *ideally, the parent is the one who decides what areas of behavior are negotiable.* That way the parent stays in the role of nurturer and guide, instead of having to react to a child who may have gotten way ahead of him and is now off the track. Another way to refer to the "river" of negotiable behavior that flows through the chart is to call it "nurture and training." To negotiate is to recognize the child's needs as well as your own and then help him become responsible and self-directing.

For example, as the child becomes more proficient in being toilet trained, the parent says: "Okay, you've been doing great. I'm going to let you start sleeping without diapers, and if you can handle it, you won't need diapers any more at night. But if you don't make it, we have to keep the diapers on."

This kind of negotiating (training) does two things:

1. It starts letting the child know he is getting older, bigger, more capable, and that now he has responsibilities he can learn to carry out on his own. If he succeeds in meeting a responsibility—in this case, toilet training—it becomes part of his domain of personal responsibility.

2. He is also aware that if he proves to not be quite ready for the responsibility, the area in question comes back into the negotiable range as logical consequences come into play: failure to stay dry means back to diapers for awhile.

As the child grows older many other parts of life come under the label "Negotiable Responsibility." Just a few examples are what he can wear, what he can eat, where he can go, what he can do, when he goes to bed. In grade school, a specific illustration of negotiating could be the child's allowance. The issue here is not whether you pay the child for doing chores or whether he gets a certain sum each week regardless of chores done or not done. The point is you start out by giving him a certain amount of money and making him responsible for how it is spent. During the elementary school years your goal is to teach him how to use spending money. If he succeeds in this, he can go on later to take care of buying his own school supplies, clothes, etc.

Granted, buying clothes is not usually something in a grade school child's domain of responsibility, but it is well within the reach of the teenager. As the chart shows, negotiating escalates at age 12 and above (note that the band labeled "Negotiable Responsibility" widens considerably). Often the junior high or high school child is in too much of a hurry for the parent. Now bedtime, curfew, money, chores, styles, driver's license, dating, etc. can become major battlegrounds. I asked one group of parents with teenagers to rate the following areas according to how much conflict and tension they were having with their children. In which of these areas do you have conflict or tension with your child? What is the root source of any tension in any of these areas?

AREA   *MUCH   SOME   LITTLE*

Music
Reading material
Food, diet
"Curfew" time

AREA	*MUCH*	*SOME*	*LITTLE*

Money (budget)
Friends
Clothes (styles)
Hair (style and length)
Transportation (car)
Leisure time
Grades
Chores
Homework
Care of room
Lifestyle and values
Dating—girlfriends, boyfriends
Other _____

In the class of parents I worked with, the following areas were marked ''some'' to ''much'': use of leisure time, grades, chores, homework, care of room. Not surprisingly, that item called ''chores'' got more checks than anything else, closely followed by homework and grades.

How did you match up? Your score may have been similar, or radically different in certain spots. For Jackie and me, curfew time caused the most trouble, particularly with our older son, Jeff. Starting in junior high and especially through high school, Jeff made a career of breaking curfew. He wasn't too fond of any rules, but curfew seemed to be his special enemy. In fact, I think there were times when the boy would wait out on the curb for twenty, thirty, or more minutes, just to be sure he was late!

We tried appealing to his maturity. (''When your mom or I know we'll be late, we phone and explain. It's the considerate thing to do.'') We tried logical consequences. (''Late again on Friday night? Can't go out next Friday.'') We even tried ''severe and unusual punishment'' (taking away the car). All to little avail. Jeff ran up so much ''you're grounded'' time that if he had served it all, he'd still be in his room.

With curfew time we never did find the key to turn the lock on Jeff's stubborn spirit. He would complain about "being tired of being treated like a little kid." And we would wonder, "Is the lad ever going to become responsible and mature?"

Maybe you don't have a problem area quite as disturbing as our "curfew crisis" was with Jeff. Or maybe you are smiling and thinking, "Oh, if only that was all I had to worry about." Every family bears its own crosses, takes its own wins and losses, and deparents at its own speed. Jeff's aversion to curfew is a good example, however, of what the deparenting ball game is all about. Sometimes you coast to victory; sometimes you go into extra innings. It depends on the child.

Kimberly, our oldest, would go to any lengths to make curfew hour. As she was finishing up her senior year in high school, she had stopped by to see her boyfriend at his job one night and the time got away. It was a week night and curfew was 11:00 P.M. She raced up the freeway and attracted the attention of one of those cars with a red light. The highway patrolman pulled her over and wanted to know, "What's the hurry?"

"It's almost 11:00 and my dad will kill me if I'm not home!" was Kim's almost tearful explanation.

The patrolman looked into the brimming blue eyes of the pretty little blonde he had stopped and imagined her ogre father crouching at the door with his cudgel. (Actually, I didn't own a cudgel; a ping-pong paddle had always sufficed, if needed, but I'd stopped using it many years before.)

"Tell you what, honey," he said as he put his ticket book away, "you follow me home. I think we can still make it. Where do you live?"

And so Kim arrived home that night, with a few minutes to spare, escorted almost to our door by the California Highway Patrol.

With Kim, the process of deparenting went quite well. We usually granted freedom and its accompanying responsibility at the right time, and she usually responded with the disciplined precision of a Chris Evert backhand. But Jeff was cut from other cloth.

We had to wait him out, but that's another story, for a later chapter.

Key Attitude #3: Letting Go

In one sense the rest of this book will deal with the art of deparenting. The attitude you need is one of *"letting go."* In a way it's a paradox. You want to nurture your child and teach responsibility, but you have to let go in order to do it.

To put it bluntly, you have to risk it. It takes courage to deparent—and a certain amount of humility. Whenever you ease up on the reins you always face the possibility that things won't turn out too well. You can end up disappointed, embarrassed, and discouraged. But it's worth it. Besides, it has to be done. It makes no difference if parents balk at deparenting; sons and daughters are rushing pell-mell to "dechild," as shown by these comments from students at a Christian university. According to our carefully planned chart, deparenting should be almost completed by the time the child is 18, 19, or 20. But in my research I found many collegians who still chafe at the parental bit.

Joyce, a freshman, said: "I'm old enough to make up my own mind, just don't worry so much. I'm not a little baby anymore. . . ."

Another freshman girl at the same school put the same thought in a colorful way: "Sometimes I feel that you look at me as an inexperienced butterfly and you are the leaves of wisdom just waiting for me to land on you and accept all your solid and unmoveable advice" (Char, 18).

And a sophomore boy added: "Treat me like a human being. I don't need you anymore. I'm independent, I can think, reason, and figure things out for myself" (Bill, 19).

These comments illustrate the tremendous pressures working on the parent-child relationship. The teenager is developing, changing, reaching for independence. You would love to give it to him, but is he ready? That is always the question. *What* do you let go of and *when*? In chapter 10 you will find some suggestions for carrying out a plan for deparenting as teenagers reach various ages and stages. It is not a final word, but it is something to bounce off of and compare as you develop a deparenting plan that can work for you. At this point, however, I hope you will take time to think about your basic attitude toward deparenting. Go over the suggestions at the end of this chapter and be painfully honest. Deparenting isn't done in a day; it's done every day as you nurture and bolster your teenager.

And, deparenting is never done twice the same way. Every child is different (witness Jeff and Kim regarding curfews). To deparent properly you must *know* your teenager—from the inside out. And that's what we'll look at in the next chapter.

FOR THOUGHT, DISCUSSION, AND ACTION

1. Take a few minutes to list areas of behavior where your teenager is completely responsible. Don't worry if you aren't sure if the list is complete. Put down as many as you can think of.

2. Now list areas where you feel things are negotiable. This may be a much longer list than the first one. The picture you are starting to get may be quite revealing.

3. Next, list areas where you believe your teenager's behavior is still completely in your domain of responsibility. Write down some specific reasons why this is so.

4. Now choose some areas where you hope your teenager can become completely responsible by a certain date. For example, will he or she get a driver's license by age 16? What will the arrangements be for use of the family car? Or will the teenager get a car of his own? If so, how is it paid for and maintained?

5. The art of deparenting and the crucial task of building self-esteem in your children go hand in hand. An excellent resource for families with younger teenagers is the *Dad's Only* newsletter, a six-page monthly publication that is loaded with ideas for building self-esteem in your children. Here's a sample:

DINNER DATE. Ask one of your teenage children out for a meal (breakfast or dinner would be best). Explain that you want him to bring along a list of three ways he would like you to show more interest in him. Develop your own list of how you would like your child to show more interest in you. Share your lists during the meal and discuss how you're both going to respond. [1]

See Notes for how to subscribe to *Dad's Only*.

6. Among the collegians I surveyed was a junior girl whose advice for her parents can easily be adapted by just about anyone with teenagers. Her words are a . . .

Short Course in Building Self-Esteem

"Show interest in my activities. Learn the rules of the sport I play, come to my games, set aside time for me, accept me."

4.

In the Way He Should Go, or in His Own Way?

"I am what I am" (Valerie, 18).

IF YOU WERE ASKED to think of one Scripture verse where God has parents especially in mind, what would you come up with? (Hint: Ephesians 6:4 doesn't count in this quiz. This verse is in the Old Testament and was written by a very wise king.)

If you thought of Proverbs 22:6, I'm not surprised. Most parents can quote it, or at least have heard of it:

"Train up a child in the way he should go. Even when he is old he will not depart from it" (NASB).

That's good advice. King Solomon didn't always follow it, but it's good advice nonetheless. Solomon even tosses in a promise to us harried parents. If we train our kids right, when they are grown, they will not depart from what we've taught them.

If you're like I was while rearing my children, you take the King James version of Proverbs 22:6 at face value. Most people do. While teaching a class of parents, I asked them what they thought Proverbs 22:6 meant.

A father with children 16, 14, 12, and 5 said: "Make sure you put forth your best effort in training your children—results come later."

A mother with an 11-year-old boy added: "Lay a foundation . . . that includes love, discipline, responsibility, and understanding through Christian training at home, church."

These are typical views of what many people think the verse

61

means. The idea is: "I, the Christian parent, know the way and it's my responsibility to train my children accordingly."

There is, however, another way to look at this verse. You get a clue from one of those little marginal notes you find in some translations of Proverbs 22:6. The New American Standard Version says in its margin: "According to his way." Dr. Charles Swindoll believes that training a child according to his way is ". . . altogether different from *your* way. God is not saying, 'Bring up a child as *you* see him.' Instead, He says, 'If you want your training to be godly and wise, observe your child, be sensitive and alert so as to discover *his* way, and adapt your training accordingly.' "[1]

Many other Christian expositors join Swindoll in this interpretation of Proverbs 22:6. For example, the Amplified Bible reads: "Train up a child in the way he should go (and in keeping with his individual gift or bent), and when he is old he will not depart from it."

The Amplified has a nice balance. There is the concept of giving the child biblical training, but as one mother of four in one of my parenting classes put it: "Treat each child as an individual with a personality of his own and train him according to his talents and disposition."

Built into the real meaning of *chahnaak*, (the Hebrew word for "train") is a vital clue about how to parent—particularly a teenager. *Chahnaak* literally means "palate" or "roof of the mouth." It suggested two ideas to the Jews:

1. There is the picture of breaking a wild stallion, which needed a rope, or bit in his mouth. The idea is that of bringing a wild spirit into submission.

2. There is also the picture of a midwife as she would dip her index finger into a saucer of tart-tasting grapes and rub the juice on the roof of a newborn child's mouth. This created a sucking sensation, or a thirst, much like biting into a dill pickle would.

Bring these two pictures together and you have something like this: To train your child properly you must see your task of bringing a wild spirit into submission by creating a thirst or taste for what you want him to know.

Lest you think this refers only to infants or younger children, the Hebrew word for "child" in the Old Testament is used in a variety of ways. It ranges from a brand new infant (1 Samuel 4) to a child in preteen years (Genesis 21) to a teenager (Genesis 37) to a person of marriageable age (Genesis 34). It's true that once a child reaches adolescence you can't train him in the same way you did in earlier years. Most of the basic molding is done, but there is still plenty of work left. If you want to see it as grinding off the rough edges, you are probably in for a struggle. If you can see it as more of a polishing, stroking kind of thing you will probably do a lot better.

What turns teenagers off is parents who come on with lectures, nagging, and patronizing all of which makes them feel: (a) like little kids, and (b) not like their own person.

Also especially galling to a teenager is to compare him to others. When asked what he wished his parents understood better about him, Loren, 14, said: "How I'm different from everyone else, and not to show me people and say, 'You should be like him.'"

The ancient Hebrews knew this—at least King Solomon did. That's why the deeper meaning of Proverbs 22:6 tells parents to train up a teenager in his own way, according to the kind of person he is.

Strange how the Bible dovetails so nicely with sound psychology. At first glance, the idea of training a child in his own way may sound like returning to the early days of Dr. Spock, with permissiveness running amuck.[2] But that can hardly be so if we remember that the Hebrews saw training a child in much the same light as breaking a wild stallion. The Jews believed in firmness, but they also believed in treating each person like the unique individual God made him.

"In his own way" does not mean giving the child (or the teenager) his own way indiscriminately. It means treating him according to how God put him (or her) together. Another mother in one of my parenting classes had obviously read Swindoll or someone with a similar view because her interpretation of Proverbs 22:6 is profound: "Train up a child according to his own temperament, learning the best way he responds to you, to life, and to God."

How Well Do You Know Your Teenager?

Some parents might say, "Too well." Others might reply: "His mind left home when he turned 13. His body is here, but I'm really not that familiar with what goes on inside it." According to many of the teenagers I talked with, they wish their parents knew them better. It's not always easy to tell who's at fault, but remarks like these are not unusual:

"Look at me as another person, more than just a child" (James, 18).

"Put yourself in my position. Remember what you felt like as a teenager. In relating, just be yourself, be natural" (Laurie, 19).

"Tell them (her parents) not to expect so much from me, so if I can't manage to do a thing to the top, they won't feel frustrated" (Ruth, 17).

Fifteen-year-old Beth wished her parents could know: "How I feel when I do something wrong and *I* know it, and *they* know it, and *God*, too, and why I feel miserable for weeks after."

And Roxanne, 14, added: "I wish they understood *me*, my personality, how I am."

As I talked with teenagers some came on strong, like Laurie ("Put yourself in *my* position . . ."). Others were more timid and hesitant like Ruth ("Tell them not to expect so much . . ."). In Beth you can see a tender conscience ("How I feel when I do something wrong . . . miserable for weeks . . .").

And so it went. We are all so different. If there is anything parents seem to know instinctively, it is that no two children are ever alike. One is quiet and studious; another hits the world running and doesn't stop. One flits about like a butterfly, the other comes on with a touch like King Kong. It is easy to sense these obvious differences, but many parents miss the tremendous significance of how their own temperaments blend or conflict with their child's.

Psychologists differ at some points, but most have agreed for a long time that people have distinct temperaments or emotional makeups. Many sophisticated studies have been done and various tests are available to give you a scientific analysis of your personality. For example, there is the Myers-Briggs Type Indicator, which can categorize you as one of 16 temperament combinations. The Keirsey Temperament Sorter is a similar kind of test, which asks questions like:

"Do you prefer to work: (a) to deadlines; (b) just "whenever."

"At parties do you: (a) stay late, with increasing energy; (b) leave early, with decreased energy."[3]

One of the simplest approaches to temperaments is based on the thinking of the Greek philosopher and physician Hippocrates, in 400 B.C. As he observed people, Hippocrates identified the extroverts and introverts, the optimists and pessimists. He came up with four basic temperaments: Sanguine, Choleric, Melancholy, and Phlegmatic. Twentieth-century psychologist Karl Jung had a similar approach to personality theory as he identified the four types as: extrovert feeling type (Sanguine); extrovert thinking type (Choleric); introvert thinking type (Melancholy); and introvert feeling type (Phlegmatic).[4]

In recent years the Sanguine, Choleric, Melancholy, and Phlegmatic temperaments theory has been popularized by Dr. Tim LaHaye, who has written *Spirit Controlled Temperament, Understanding the Male Temperament* and *Transformed Temperaments*.[5] Florence Littauer read LaHaye's books, studied the temperaments and revitalized her marriage with a better understanding of herself and her husband Fred. For almost fifteen years she has taught the four temperaments to women's groups across the United States and in Canada. The following brief descriptions of Sanguine, Choleric, Melancholy, and Phlegmatic are based on her workshop notes, as well as her excellent book, *Personality Plus*, a study in how to understand yourself and others through a knowledge of the temperaments.

Keep in mind that these descriptions are not precise, nor do all of the characteristics apply to everyone in every case. All of us are unique blends of characteristics. Usually, however, people have strong tendencies toward one temperament or another.

Sanguines: Happy, Chatty, Forgetful

Sanguines are the extroverts who are optimistic and always talking. Sanguines are story tellers, life-of-the-party types who are emotional, demonstrative, and enthusiastic. They bubble with cheer in their animated expressive way.

On the negative side, Sanguines can exaggerate and dwell on trivia, but seldom remember names. Their loud voices and laughter can turn some people off and they sometimes appear egotistical or phony because of being so outgoing. They can get angry easily and often seem childish, in need of "growing up."

Sanguines make friends easily and love people. They thrive on compliments, don't hold grudges and like spontaneity. Sanguines also like center stage and crave popularity. They like to get the credit and dominate conversations by interrupting others and not listening.

As parents, Sanguines have positive traits that make home fun. They can turn disaster into humor and are liked by their child's friends because they are so outgoing and friendly. Weaknesses in Sanguine parents may include not being organized, which may keep the home in a state of frenzy. Sanguines are forgetful and can miss appointments with other family members. They are also prone to not listen to the whole story and jump to conclusions too easily.

Sanguine parents may also need to guard against trying to act a little "too hip" around their teenagers. I talked with Jamie, a high school junior, who described his mom as, "A very open lady. She wears tight jeans and sometimes she embarrasses me with her driving and her talking . . . she talks quite a bit. One day when I was playing in a baseball game she rode up on my little brother's Mongoose dirt bike. And she couldn't understand why I walked away from her."

Teenagers who are Sanguines are often in the popular crowd at school. They are likely to make cheerleader, homecoming queen or king, and the lead in the class play. They often date a lot. Their energy and enthusiasm mixes with charm and wit. It all adds up to a charisma that looks great on the surface. Sanguines like to get by on their charm and aren't always that good at following through or meeting obligations and deadlines. They count on feelings more than thinking and can be undisciplined about things like keeping phone calls at a reasonable length or keeping their rooms reasonably neat.

Cholerics: Leaders, Drivers, Dominating

Cholerics are also extroverts and optimists, but their goal in life is to "get it done." They are born leaders, always ready for action. Strong willed and decisive, Cholerics ooze with confidence and seldom get discouraged as they go through life getting things organized, making changes, and righting wrongs.

On the minus side, their powerful style can make others see them as bossy, impatient, quick tempered, and unable to relax. They love controversy and competition and would rather die than lose. They can be inflexible and unsympathetic and are not known for handing out lots of compliments.

As parents, Cholerics run a tight ship with a masterful hand. They establish goals, motivate everyone to get on the ball and always (well, almost always) know the right answer to the problem. Choleric parents can have problems because they are often workaholic types who are too busy for the family. When they are around they tend to dominate and get impatient with less-than-perfect performance.

Ron, a high-school freshman, described his dad as always helping him out and always showing interest in his participation in track and cross country. Sometimes at home, however, Ron remembers when ". . . we'll be out working, Dad and I . . . he's a workaholic, and so I always have to be with him. We'll be out there doing something, and if he tells me to do something and I don't do it exactly the way he does it—I may do it a different way—he gets mad and just yells. And then it will be okay after that.''

Quick-thinking Choleric parents are tempted to answer for others (a rather deadly habit when trying to get a teenager to express himself). It's hard to relax around a Choleric parent and some kids even go into depression if the pressure mounts too high.

Because they are so goal oriented and see the big picture so well, Choleric teenagers are often looked to by their schoolmates for leadership. The teenage Choleric is the kind who captains the football team or gets elected to class office (if he doesn't turn too many people off with impatience or bossiness).

At home, Choleric young people can be rude and tactless and may try to dominate and manipulate their brothers and sisters. They can be too independent and may come on extra strong with that typical teenage characteristic of knowing everything and being able to do everything better. They often have a hard time saying "I'm sorry."

Melancholies: Thinkers, Perfectionists, Sensitive

Melancholies are the deep and thoughtful people. Many of them are talented, creative types, gifted in music or art. Others lean toward the detail side of life; they like graphs, charts, and figures and enjoy research and analysis.

Melancholies are often sensitive to others, self-sacrificing and conscientious. Their serious and purposeful approach to life makes them see the glass half empty rather than half full. They can easily become moody and depressed as they center too much on themselves and their feelings.

As parents, Melancholies set high standards. They want everything done right and are usually meticulous housekeepers. They sacrifice for their children and encourage them to do well in school. But when these parents tend to push too hard, they can discourage their kids with goals and standards that seem to be out of reach. Melancholies can be too meticulous, too schedule oriented. When things don't go like clockwork they may sulk, don the martyr's shroud, or try to send everyone in the family on a guilt trip.

Often content with a low profile, Melancholy young people don't make the big splash at school that Sanguines and Cholerics do. Melancholy teenagers make friends cautiously, but once they do find a friend they are faithful and devoted. They are good listeners and become known among schoolmates for being concerned, compassionate counselors.

At home, as well as at school, Melancholy youngsters may seem withdrawn and remote, "off in another world." They can be suspicious and are often skeptical when praised or complimented. Critical by nature, they can become antagonistic. Forgiveness is not their strong suit and they often seek revenge for wrongs done them by family members. Most teenagers are often stereotyped as moody and changeable, but Melancholies can have special problems that need extra understanding.

Phlegmatics: Calm, Easy Going, Indecisive

Phlegmatics are introverts and pessimists who often come in a plain brown wrapper. They would rather watch than do, switch than fight. Phlegmatics are often known as "not having an enemy in the world." Easy going, relaxed, calm, cool, and collected all apply to Phlegmatics. Other good descriptions are well balanced, consistent, and quiet. They keep emotions hidden but are usually sympathetic and kind.

The flip side of the Phlegmatic coin reveals some weaknesses that can give them trouble. They can be so low key they appear unenthusiastic. Sometimes that laid-back exterior covers worries and fears. Phlegmatics are often indecisive and aren't known for volunteering for responsibilities. Phlegmatics can appear easy going, but sometimes they can be hiding a stubborn selfish streak.

At work, Phlegmatics are the competent steady types who haven't missed a day in five years. They are good under pressure and do what they're told, but it is usually wise to have them work under a strong leader. Phlegmatics are not goal oriented. It's hard to get them moving and they resent being pushed. The undisciplined Phlegmatic can be lazy and careless and would rather watch than work.

Phlegmatics have the basic tools to be excellent parents. They don't get upset easily, can take the bad with the good, and are seldom in a hurry. All this is perfect for rearing children, especially when they are young. Phlegmatic parents may have difficulty when children hit teenage years, however, because they tend to be lax on discipline and disorganized. Phlegmatic parents can often wind up in the permissive category that allows the teenager free rein and free roam. The result is usually problems for the parents, and sometimes for the teenager.

I talked with one high-school girl whose parents were much older than usual—in their sixties. Their entire attitude was one of "Do what you want. We don't care." The girl felt so uncared for she finally ran away and wound up staying in a foster home where the father was a policeman, and definitely not a Phlegmatic.

Like Melancholies, Phlegmatics are usually part of the background at school. Phlegmatic teenagers may have quite a few friends or practically none at all. If their positive traits surface, friends will be attracted because they like someone who is easy to get along with, who never argues over what to do or where to go.

Phlegmatics are also often good listeners and possessed of a dry sense of humor. They often pair off with Choleric leader types who are looking for followers. Some Phlegmatic kids, however, may come on so softly they are considered dull or boring. At home, the pure Phlegmatic can have problems, especially with a Choleric father who may see him as indifferent, lazy, and unwilling to change.[6]

Why Bother with Temperaments?

Why do I bother with all this stuff on the four temperaments? Because it can be invaluable in helping you understand yourself, your spouse, *and* your teenagers. To repeat, the above sketches of the four temperaments are not to be taken as precise psychological profiles. Frankly, it is difficult to describe anyone with pinpoint accuracy, no matter what your approach might be. No one is completely one temperament or another. We are all intricate blends that make each of us unique individuals.

According to Florence Littauer and Tim LaHaye, who both have tests to determine temperament, most people test out with one major temperament and one or two fairly strong subtemperaments. For example, according to Littauer's word association test (see pages 74–75), I test out mostly Choleric with a good dose of Melancholy and a little Sanguine. My wife comes out mostly Melancholy with a strong secondary trait of Phlegmatic. This helps us understand why I can get impatient and eventually depressed and why she is the meticulous housekeeper who will stay up late finishing chores with grim determination. It also helps me see why my Choleric tendency to be goal oriented and "overdirective" brings out the Phlegmatic stubbornness in my little wife, who isn't always that receptive to my ideas.

And so it goes. Understanding the temperaments, even in a rudimentary fashion, gives us a tremendous tool for understanding each other and learning to appreciate each other's good points.

When you apply the temperaments to parent-child relationships their value is obvious. If you learn, for example, that your son is strongly Phlegmatic while you are primarily Choleric, it might help to explain why you are constantly complaining that he is lazy and he is constantly wishing you would get off his back. Or, perhaps you are a Sanguine who greets each new day with enthusiasm and the certain knowledge that you're going to have fun. No wonder you can't quite understand why your Melancholy daughter is prone to fits of tears and depression, has never been a really happy child, and is content to spend long hours daydreaming.

The possible combinations are endless. We have used the Littauer test on all our children and it fits each of their personalities almost perfectly. Kim, for example, came out slightly more Choleric than I am, with a strong Melancholy subtrait. No wonder Kim has been organizing all of us since she was a toddler. My wife still recalls the day she put 4-year-old Kim out in our fenced back yard to play. In two minutes she was knocking at the door. "What's the matter, honey?" my wife asked. "The gate is open," Kim reported matter-of-factly. "You better shut it so I won't get out."

In high school Kim developed her organizing skills in many ways. She took over the grocery list and often shopped for her mother. She headed up the committees for homecoming and the prom, and she also had a thing for organizing desks. She often straightened the desks of favorite teachers and valiantly tried to keep mine neat as well. It was futile, however, and she finally gave me a kiss, pronounced me hopeless and left me to what I happily call "creative chaos."

Jeff, our middle child, has turned out to be the charmer who can talk his way into or out of almost anything. I sometimes marvel at his verbal skills and quick tongue, but it should be no surprise, because he is half Sanguine, with a strong dose of Choleric thrown in. Jeff loves people, relating, talking, sharing. He struggled during his first semester in college, but since then has been making slow but steady progress with academia. Books, you see, don't talk, and it is always tempting to wind up down at a local coffee shop "studying with a friend."

Jeff also struggles toward the virtue of neatness, but not too hard. He is well groomed personally, but his room usually looks like the bargain counter five minutes after the sale starts. Making his bed was always a bone of contention between our Sanguine son and his mother. He and Jackie would go round and round. Jackie tried positive reinforcement, logical consequences, and even "special pacts"—all to no avail.

I supported her efforts but rejoiced when she finally accepted the differences between her son's values and her own Melancholy meticulousness. Now she either shuts his door or makes his bed herself, and she is praying that he will find a wife willing to do the same. She says: "When I think of all the ways so many kids are messed up today, an unmade bed is a minor point, and I'm not going to let it come between us."

Todd, our youngest, is a no-nonsense young man just out of high school. The reverse of Jeff, he is half Choleric, with a strong streak of Sanguine. This helps explain why he sees himself as adventurous, competitive, daring, and confident. He has plenty of scars to prove it. He also admits to impatience, frankness, and occasional spells of irritability. For example, Todd was the one who organized the purchase of a gift for his basketball coach at a year-end awards banquet. He also collected money for flowers when the coach's wife had a baby daughter. When we noted his thoughtfulness his only comment was an exasperated, "If I hadn't done it, no one else would have!"

Key Attitude #4: Acceptance

Proverbs 22:6 teaches the main theme of this chapter—*acceptance*. The temperament tests introduced a whole new concept of acceptance for Jackie and me. Now we see why one child can be conscientious while the other one seems to be uncaring about following through on details. When you begin to understand your child's temperament you can take some of his imperfections a lot less personally.

Try the Florence and Fred Littauer Temperament Test on pages 74–75. Test yourself and then give it to your spouse and your teenagers. (Older teenagers are perfectly capable of the word association that is necessary; younger children might need help with definitions.) After learning clues to everyone's temperament, talk about it together. It can be a great way of bringing Proverbs 22:6 to life in a new and different light. Each of us secretly wishes people "could be more like me." But people aren't just like you. We are all different and like being dealt with "in our own way"—according to our individual bent.

Among the teenagers I surveyed, 16-year-old Jennie put it beautifully when she told her parents: "I love you. I am a growing person that needs lots of guidance and counseling. I am getting to know myself and what kind of life I want to lead. I believe I have a lot of great qualities that you might not have seen and want to share them with you if you will let me. I want you to be my friend."

THE TEMPERAMENT TEST

This word association test was developed by Florence and Fred Littauer and has been used with thousands of participants in their "Personality Plus" seminars. In each of the following rows of four words across, place an "X" in front of the *one word* that *most often applies* to you. Be sure to mark one word on each line, even if, in some cases, the choices do not fit you exactly. From each set of four words, pick the one that *comes closest* to describing you. For instructions on how to score the test, see Appendix 3, page 200.

1	___ Animated	___ Adventurous	___ Analytical	___ Adaptable
2	___ Persistent	___ Playful	___ Persuasive	___ Peaceful
3	___ Submissive	___ Self-Sacrificing	___ Sociable	___ Strong-Willed
4	___ Considerate	___ Controlled	___ Competitive	___ Convincing
5	___ Refreshing	___ Respectful	___ Reserved	___ Resourceful
6	___ Satisfied	___ Sensitive	___ Self-Reliant	___ Spirited
7	___ Planner	___ Patient	___ Positive	___ Promoter
8	___ Sure	___ Spontaneous	___ Scheduled	___ Shy
9	___ Orderly	___ Obliging	___ Outspoken	___ Optimistic
10	___ Friendly	___ Faithful	___ Funny	___ Forceful
11	___ Daring	___ Delightful	___ Diplomatic	___ Detailed
12	___ Cheerful	___ Consistent	___ Cultured	___ Confident
13	___ Idealistic	___ Independent	___ Inoffensive	___ Inspiring
14	___ Demonstrative	___ Decisive	___ Dry Humor	___ Deep
15	___ Mediator	___ Musical	___ Mover	___ Mixes Easily
16	___ Thoughtful	___ Tenacious	___ Talker	___ Tolerant
17	___ Listener	___ Loyal	___ Leader	___ Lively

#			
18	Contented	Chief	Cute
19	Perfectionist	Permissive	Popular
20	Bouncy	Bold	Balanced
21	Brassy	Bossy	Blank
22	Undisciplined	Unsympathetic	Unforgiving
23	Reluctant	Resentful	Repetitious
24	Fussy	Fearful	Frank
25	Impatient	Insecure	Interrupts
26	Unpopular	Uninvolved	Unaffectionate
27	Headstrong	Haphazard	Hesitant
28	Plain	Pessimistic	Permissive
29	Angered Easily	Aimless	Alienated
30	Naive	Negative Attitude	Nonchalant
31	Worrier	Withdrawn	Wants Credit
32	Too Sensitive	Tactless	Talkative
33	Doubtful	Disorganized	Depressed
34	Inconsistent	Introvert	Indifferent
35	Messy	Moody	Manipulative
36	Slow	Stubborn	Skeptical
37	Loner	Lord-over-others	Loud
38	Sluggish	Suspicious	Scatter-brained
39	Revengeful	Restless	Rash
40	Compromising	Critical	Changeable

Taken from the *After Every Wedding Comes a Marriage Workbook*, copyright 1981, Harvest House Publishers, Eugene, Oregon. Used by permission.

FOR THOUGHT, DISCUSSION, AND ACTION

1. Can you think of some specific things you are doing to train your teenager ''in his own way''—according to his God-given temperament, gifts, and traits? What are you doing to enhance his strengths? To help him with weaknesses?

2. Analyze the statements:

> Your relationship to your teenager is more
> important than your dignity or pride.

> Attitudes are more important in shaping a
> good relationship than standards or skills.

Do you agree or disagree? How will it affect your behavior toward your teenager?

3. Do more study on the temperaments.

As mentioned in this chapter, a knowledge of temperaments has enormous potential for improving your relationship with your spouse and with your teenager. To learn more about how the temperaments work in a family, get a copy of Florence Littauer's excellent book, *Personality Plus* (Fleming H. Revell, 1982). After describing your personality profile, the book goes on to look at your personality potential (your temperament strengths) and then presents a personality plan (a way to overcome your personal weaknesses). A final important section of the book gives you personality principles for improving relationships with others. *Personality Plus* is loaded with practical illustrations, many of them family oriented. For other good books to read in this area, see ''Resources for Parents,'' Appendix 2, page 195.

4. Tips on ''Temperament Living'':

If you are a Sanguine parent: cut down on your talking and learn to really listen . . . be more interested in what others are doing and thinking . . . remember that everyone doesn't see the world through your rosy glasses . . . work on being more dependable and following through.

If you have a Sanguine teenager: realize Sanguines have trouble following through . . . give as much flexibility as you can, Sanguines dislike structure . . . be patient with forgotten appointments or tardiness . . . give lots of praise, it is a special need for Sanguines . . . reassure yourself that your son or daughter means well, and is not trying to drive you to drink . . . be thankful for your happy Sanguine and relax.

If you are a Choleric parent: work at not coming on so strong . . . make an effort to give your teenager compliments (one or two sincere ones a day, if possible) . . . bite your tongue if you are tempted to say, "I told you so" . . . let your teenager do a job his way, even if it's not perfect . . . keep advice to yourself until asked, then work on giving it tactfully, not with both barrels.

If you have a Choleric teenager: be patient, but firm with impatience and loss of temper . . . realize that Cholerics are not known for tact or compassion, they can hurt feelings without meaning to . . . be aware they are no-nonsense people who set goals and want to reach them . . . since they are born leaders, let them lead when possible.

If you are a Melancholy parent: read Philippians 4:6–8 every day and keep a positive outlook as much as possible . . . work at not taking everything too personally . . . learn to accept imperfect people (especially your kids) . . . check to be sure you aren't becoming a slave to the family, always sacrificing for everyone else, which can give you a martyr complex . . . force yourself to talk, but don't expect everyone to think as you do.

If you have a Melancholy teenager: handle with care, remembering that Melancholies are especially sensitive and have a pessimistic outlook on life . . . go slow with the "good cheer" and "positive thinking," these often make Melancholies feel worse! . . . if you spot signs of depression, gently prod them to get up and get going . . . throw in a few extra "I love you's" and "You're doing great's," Melancholies like reassurance and praise . . . accept their desire for silence at times and don't bug them with erratic schedules or being late.

If you are a Phlegmatic parent: work at being more decisive and enthused . . . set goals you can reach and go after them . . . try something new . . . avoid procrastinating and just watching others . . . stay easy going, but be sure to keep going!

If you have a Phlegmatic teenager: don't be discouraged by lack of enthusiasm for life . . . realize Phlegmatics need motivating, help your son or daughter set realistic goals, give rewards when goals are reached . . . force your Phlegmatic to accept responsibilities and make decisions, even if it's a bit painful at times . . . never call your Phlegmatic "lazy" (even if it's true), be positive, and appreciate a family member with an even, predictable disposition.

Unit II: Communication

Communicating with Your Teenagers—
Is Not Always Easy

A second major theme that rings loud and clear when talking with teenagers about their parents is communication. To be more exact, it is "lack of listening." The word listen *comes up again and again and many teenagers claim their parents just aren't doing it. Parents could easily fire back the same charge and that would make it a communication stand-off.*

In the next three chapters we'll grapple with the causes and cures of communication problems as we look at:

. . . several lethal communication-killers and their antidotes.

. . . the "lack of listening" disease . . . is it terminal?

. . . the secret weapon every parent needs.

. . . the deadliest enemy of every family.

. . . the equation that can solve family arguments.

. . . the key attitudes of thoughtfulness, perseverance, forgiveness.

5.

Communication Needs
Tender Loving Care

"Don't be so stubborn . . . please listen!" (Kelli, 19).

WHEN I ASKED TEENAGERS, "How well do you communicate with your parents?" their answers showed everything from eagerness and longing:

"I wish that I could talk to them, because I never can talk personally to them" (Dandi, 15).

"I love them and if we could listen to each other more, perhaps we would understand one another as well" (Judie, 18).

"I'm confused often, just help me. I've often tried to show my love, but I'm finding it hard" (Jennifer, 15).

. . . to frustration and regret:

"There is very little communication and I'm sorry" (Ralph, 16).

"When I'm talking they should listen and not ask ten minutes later, 'What?' Then they would understand why I get annoyed with them when I must repeat myself" (Debbie, 17).

"I'll try and tell them something and they'll keep saying, 'OK! OK!' like they could care less . . ." (Rhonda, 14).

It's hopeful to note that many young people are well aware that the lack of communication isn't all on the parents' side. In my survey of hundreds of teenagers I asked:

81

The biggest single barrier preventing good communication between parents and teenagers is:

a. parents think they know it all.
b. teenagers think they know it all.
c. parents don't want to admit they're wrong.

The answer chosen by almost half of all *teenage* respondents was "Teenagers think they know it all."

I've asked parents' classes this same question and a large number of *parents* answered with: "Parents think they know it all."

Many parents chose to write in their own answers, including:

"Poor listening . . . not starting early enough trying to communicate . . . tension . . . parents talk but don't listen . . . busyness . . . expecting too much . . . parents too concerned with own wants."

Some other write-ins from the same class included: "Lack of honesty about feelings and concerns . . . can't tell when son is telling the truth . . . too much lecturing—not enough discussion . . . nonlistening (on teenager's part) just to get the session over with."

And so it goes. The barriers are there—some erected by the teenager and others by the parents. Communication needs tender loving care, but in many homes it is abused, trampled, and killed daily. "Communication Killers" come in all shapes and sizes. In his Parent Effectiveness Training course, Thomas Gordon lists the Dirty Dozen, which includes: ordering and commanding, warning and threatening, moralizing and preaching, name calling and ridiculing.[1] In their excellent course entitled *Building Positive Teen-Parent Relationships,* Norman Wright and Rex Johnson offer their own version of a dirty dozen, which includes: not thinking before you speak, not listening, no eye contact, abusive talk, withheld words, and silence.[2]

Communication Killers usually take the form of words, which are formed hastily or without thought. There are many ways to describe these verbal missiles. Following are six garden variety Communication Killers. They all originate in the same place: a tongue that is not under control. The apostle James said it all: ". . . the tongue is a small thing, but what enormous damage it can do . . ." (James 3:5, TLB).

Gunslinger Words Can Blow You Away

"Gunslinger Words" are the kind we use when we shoot from the hip. They are the little bullets we fire when tempted to be cutting, sarcastic, cynical, or grouchy:

"Hi, Tubby, been in the fridge again?"
"Going out with your punk friends tonight?"
"Good grief, how can you be such an idiot?"

As one high schooler told me, "Then when I do admit I was wrong about something or say I'm sorry, they cut me down. They say, 'Oh, she admitted she was wrong? Mark that on a calendar . . .' or something like that. And it makes me feel bad and makes me not want to talk with them" (Kim, 17).

Anyone who lives in a family knows all about Gunslinger Words. They inflame, incite, provoke. We'll look further at this Communication Killer in chapter 7, which deals with anger. Meanwhile, it might help to remember that Proverbs 18:21 tells us: "Death and life are in the power of the tongue" (KJV). And, a paraphrase of Jesus' well-known warning about living by the sword also applies: "He who lives by Gunslinger Words sees communication die by same."

Defensive Words—Always on the Tip of the Tongue

Some parents might be thinking, "I seldom use Gunslinger Words—it's my *teenager* who is usually handing out the sarcasm or grouchies." This can well be the case, and if so, the parent has to beware of counterattacking with "Defensive Words" like: "Don't get smart with me, young man," or "You're a fine one to talk. You've got plenty of shaping up to do yourself, and furthermore . . ."

One of my biggest challenges as a parent has been learning to bite Defensive Words off the tip of my tongue. Because we have always encouraged our children to speak their minds, they sometimes come on strong. When that happens I have often invoked another wise saying I picked up somewhere years ago: "The difference between a happy relationship and a mediocre one is three or four things a day left unsaid." Tying in quite nicely with that idea is Proverbs 13:3: "Self-control means controlling the tongue! A quick retort can ruin everything" (TLB).

I have also observed that my teenagers would sometimes use aggressive remarks, teasing, or criticism as a way of initiating conversation. Sometimes you have to filter out what is really meant. If all you hear is a jab or left hook that threatens your authority or ego you're likely to come back with a counterpunch of your own and communication is down for the count.

There is, of course, always the problem of the teenager going well over the line into the area known as "smart mouth." Every parent has his or her line and when it's crossed there are several responses you can make.

It's easy to say, "I'm the parent, there will be none of that," and then fire away with your own Gunslinger or Defensive Words. This usually achieves: (a) icy silence (b) heated uproar (i.e. war).

A more positive approach is called "active listening." What are the feelings behind your teenager's words? You might ask, "It sounds as if you are bugged . . . tell me more." (For more on this technique, see chapter 6.)

If the whole thing is a bit beyond your patience or endurance, use the simple "I" message: "I can't handle that kind of remark. Let's both calm down and start over." (For more on the "I" message, see chapter 9.)

Discouraging Words Kill Self-Esteem

"Discouraging Words" often come from parents in the form of put-downs like: "That's nothing special . . . the first part was okay, but you never seem to remember . . . you always seem to blow it. . . ."

Note the presence of those two deadly discouragers: "never" and "always." Joe, a 17-year-old high school junior I talked to, knows the feeling: "A lot of times at my house I'm supposed to do certain stuff and I'll forget once to do it, like one or two days in a row, and all of a sudden—'Well, you *never* do this, you *never* do that . . . you're just getting lazy.' "

Joe's parents weren't present to give their side, but it's not hard to understand how they could slip into the "never/always" trap. Teenagers do forget; they do repeat the same mistakes. Perhaps you identify at least in part with a father who attended one of my parenting classes. He has a son, 15, and a daughter, 12, and when asked to write one thing he would like to have them both know, he said: "I've been tough on you at times and required a lot of you. You have learned a lot and will do well on your own. I love you and what I do and have done to and for you is for your own good. Thank you for forgiving me when I'm wrong, as I do for you."

Breathes there a parent who has not uttered, at least once, "I did it for their own good"? But even as we say the words, we aren't so sure, because we can remember all those things that were done or said "for our own good." Sometimes they helped, but there were plenty of times when they didn't.

It seems to come back to that elusive quality called balance. There is definitely a place for correction. Paul mentions the idea in Ephesians 6:4 when he talks about bringing up children in the "admonition" of the Lord. But it's so easy to slip into the critical zone where your words aren't heard, they're simply absorbed, like punches in a boxing match. Many teenagers would like to direct their parents to the words of the apostle Paul in Romans 14:13: ". . . stop turning critical eyes on one another. If we must be critical, let us be critical of our own conduct" (Phillips).

Rightly or wrongly, many teenagers feel they are under constant scrutiny and that no matter how they try they can't please their parents. What a lot of them would settle for is a word or two of encouragement—the kind that has their feelings in mind, instead of their parent's values. For example, teenagers often hear, "You can do it . . . study hard and get an 'A' " or "I know you'll make it, I have *confidence* in you!"

The problem with these well-intentioned exhortations is they have a string attached. They say, "Achieve, and then you are approved." Sue, a college junior, remembers teenage years over-shadowed by "a lot of heavy expectations" from her parents. "I wanted to be worthwhile," she recalled. "I wanted to know I was okay. But I was only okay if I got good grades, said the right things, acted the right way. I always wanted to be accepted. Some-times what I said was off the wall, but I didn't know that at the time. I needed to know that what I was saying was important, that it wasn't wrong, that it was something worthwhile, and I never really felt that."

Sue's comments are a classic mini-lesson on how *not* to build a teenager's self-esteem. She—and a lot of other young people—would agree with a slight paraphrase of Proverbs 25:11: "A word of encouragement is like apples of gold in settings of silver."[3]

Double Meaning, Double Trouble

A more subtle, but just as damaging, enemy of communication is the "Double Message." These are the vague remarks that are heard at different levels, or on different wavelengths. Key phrases in Double Messages are, "I guess so," or "We'll see," or "Later on, perhaps." I learned the hard way that when my teenagers asked me if they could go somewhere or do a certain thing and I responded with, "Maybe . . . we'll see," I had just said "Yes" as far as they were concerned.

According to my survey, I'm not alone with this problem. Joe, the high school junior quoted a few paragraphs back, reports: "Like when I say, 'Can I go somewhere?' They say, 'Oh, I guess so.' So I say, 'Well, don't you want me to go?' And they say, 'Just go, you already asked, you don't want to stay around the house.' And I tell them there's nothing to do at the house. It happens a lot. I want to know if I can do something or if we are all going to do this or that and they say, 'I don't know . . . we'll see.'"

Norm Wright and Rex Johnson make a good point when they

observe that it's easy to use Double Messages while trying to avoid a confrontation.[4] Sometimes we are weary or in a hurry and we don't want any hassle. The ideal approach is to "speak the truth in love," a sound idea that is often quoted out of context from Ephesians 4:15. Paul is talking about sharing the truth of the gospel, but the idea certainly applies to being honest in primarily personal relationships. Like most good ideas it is easy to quote, hard to do, but worthwhile.

To speak the truth in love is to send a single, not a double, message. Single messages may be greeted by moans and pained looks, but they are less apt to be misunderstood. For example, when not sure if you want to grant permission or agree to a request simply say, "I can't give you a definite answer right now. I will let you know (in half an hour, tonight, next Friday, etc.)."

The whole matter of Double Messages gets still more involved when the teenager sends you one of his own, like: "What do you think of my car?" "Does this color go with these pants?" "Oh, I just can't do anything right!" All of these can be a teenager's way of sending a message that is really asking: "Am I okay? Do you like me? Am I worthwhile?"

A good rule of thumb is to be honest but use a lot of love and tact. When teenagers send messages asking for reassurance and acceptance, it's a great time to practice active listening, a skill described more fully in chapter 6.

Double Messages aren't easy to avoid, especially when you realize that everyone is hearing what he or she wants to hear. With all those wives and children, King Solomon was well acquainted with the problem. Maybe that's why he wrote: "How wonderful it is to be able to say the right thing at the right time" (Prov. 15:23, TLB).

Nagging Parts the Best of Friends

The teenagers I surveyed complained most about "Nagging Words," which their parents might prefer to interpret as "just reminding them of their responsibilities." Parents feel they have a perfectly legitimate right to remind the kids to clean up their rooms, take out the garbage, do their homework or whatever the teenager is not doing or taking too long to do. But from the teenager's side, it's nagging.

Jeff, 17, said: "Try not to be so picky about my being home on time. Basically if you don't do exactly what they want, how they want it done, and when they want it done, they get so mad, and I would like to get that one point across to them!"

Melanie, 18, said, "Let me be more independent—don't nag me constantly."

Lisa, 18, added, "It's like they're never satisfied. It drives me nuts. No matter what I do, they want something more."

Judy, 15, says, "Definitely . . . nagging from my Mom. She tells me to do something, then a few minutes later, 'Remember. . . .' Then a few minutes later, etc. etc."

What can parents do to avoid the label, "nag"? In some cases, probably not a whole lot, particularly if their teenager's attitude is extremely touchy. For example, Chris, 14, describes his parents as, "Don't, Don't, Don't, No! No! No! Stop! Stop! Stop! NAG! NAG! NAG!!!"

As someone said so aptly, "There is nothing wrong with teenagers that telling them won't aggravate."[5] To keep aggravation levels down, however, here are some practical ideas:

1. Be sure you know when you are reminding and when it turns to nagging. Reminding is done in a friendly, hang-loose way; nagging has a different pitch to it and usually includes faultfinding that irritates your teenager.

2. Check to see if nagging is actually a habit with you. Perhaps your teenager is "playing games with your head" (as he might be prone to put it). If you find that you constantly have to repeat what you are saying, or that you just don't seem to have your child's attention, it may be time for a change.

3. Get your teenager's attention when you are talking to him. Establish eye contact; don't try to communicate from across the room, from the next room or around a corner (all favorite communication styles of many teenagers).

4. Be specific about what needs to be done, and *be brief*. Re-

member the chief teenage beef that was discussed in chapter 1: Parents talk too much and repeat everything over and over.

5. Be sure your teenager understands your request. This is sometimes tricky because a common response to "Have you got it?" is often, "Yeah, yeah, do you think I'm some kind of *dummy*?" True, some requests don't need any check. "Please take out the garbage" is fairly clear and unmistakable. But "Please run these errands for me," may take some discussion, depending on what you need and where it is.

6. Try to get a commitment on when the request will be carried out. This too can be delicate ground, because you don't want it to sound like an ultimatum. Sometimes the situation calls for a deadline; but in many cases there is leeway to allow the teenager to set his own schedule. I have learned this is very important to Todd, my 18-year-old. For example, he is responsible for cutting the lawn. Often the lawn grows a bit long and Todd needs a reminder:

"The lawn's getting pretty long."

"Yep."

"Can you cut it sometime this week?"

"I guesso—got alotta work on my truck. . . ."

"Well, how about by Friday or Saturday?"

"Okay."

Granted, this approach takes a few seconds longer, but it creates that all-important atmosphere where my teenager has some control over the situation and he can choose—to some extent—when he will do the job requested of him. (Come to think of it, I rather like to be treated the same way.)

The above ideas may work better with one teenager than another.[6] Sometimes you just have to wait the kid out. Patience is probably the best weapon to avoid the nagging syndrome. Your teenager may be trying to see how long it will take you to blow your cool. If you are in a nagging pattern, it is probably the result of some kind of values conflict between you and your teenager. Something is important to you, but not to him—and vice versa.

Confront the issue and make a plan to resolve the conflict with positive reinforcement or logical consequences. Praise your son or daughter when possible, but don't settle for piddling around. It is one thing for your teenager to piddle with a certain chore or to forget it altogether, all the while assured that the only consequence is having Mom or Dad harp (nag) about it again. But it is another matter for your teenager to know that if the chore is not done, any number of reasonable consequences can occur: a cut in allowance or TV time, no going out the next weekend, etc. Just be sure that you talk all this over with your teenager and that he or she is part of whatever you decide. (For more on setting consequences, see chapter 9.)

Oh yes, one more thing. If your relationship to your teenager is important to you at all, remember: "Love forgets mistakes. Nagging about them parts the best of friends" (Prov. 17:9, TLB).

Thoughtless Words Take Little Thought

In a way, all of the above Communication Killers could come under the label, "Thoughtless Words." To shoot from the hip takes little thought, as does defensive counterpunching to protect your pride. To discourage, to send double messages, to nag—none of these require much reflection. There is, however, one particular brand of Thoughtless Words that a large percentage of teenagers mentioned to me. It is summed up in Proverbs 18:13: "What a shame—yes, how stupid!—to decide before knowing the facts!" (TLB).

If anything drives a teenager up the wall it is to be confronted by a parent who doesn't want to listen to any explanations (for being late, why a task is not done, why a grade is so low, etc.). I have heard these typical comments from many teenagers:

"Please listen to everything I say before you think of a reply" (Stephanie, 19).

"They just turn you off and stick with their own ideas, not letting the teenager put his point across" (Eugene, 16).

"Please try to understand the things I do—don't reprimand me before listening to my side of the problem" (Pamela, 19).

"In a disagreement they won't listen to the other side of a story. Being parents, they accept their side of the story" (Loren, 14).

Lisa, 18-year-old freshman at a Christian university, feels both her parents are adept at jumping to conclusions. "I'll start telling them a story, like what happened in school one day, like maybe I had to miss a class. 'YOU missed a class?' And then they'll just start going on. 'YOU know better than that. . . .' Maybe I had to, you know, help out a teacher, but they don't let me finish. They just keep going. That really irritates me."

There are, of course, many other ways to use Thoughtless Words. Opportunities are unlimited, or so it seems for me. One evening, Jackie, Todd, and I were eating dinner and the subject turned to a girl Todd might ask for a date. Todd asked his mother if she liked a certain girl and while she searched for a tactful way to reply, I thought I would be helpful by explaining one thing that bothered her about this particular girl.

"Mom doesn't like it too well when girls repeatedly call here to talk to you."

Communication froze and I got icy stares from all directions. My little wife is one of the few brown-eyed people I know who can give you a frosty look that will rival any pair of blue eyes on this planet.

Did King Solomon ever have nights like that? Maybe so. He once wrote: "Don't talk so much. You keep putting your foot in your mouth" (Prov. 10:19, TLB).

Key Attitude #5: Thoughtfulness

There are many more Communication Killers than the six we've looked at here, and they are all linked in some way to not thinking, not caring, not listening. As a matter of fact, the entire next chapter is devoted to curing the "lack of listening" disease that afflicts most of us.

The opposite of any Communication Killer is *thoughtfulness*, which blends nicely with words like *kind, gracious, considerate,* and *helpful*. The battle is never done, but with effort you can win one once in a while, as these teenage comments prove:

"I like my dad because he's funny and kind, and all my friends like him a lot. I like my mom because she likes to do some things other moms don't do any more" (Judy, 15).

"Thank you for letting me be me, and letting me realize who I am. I realize that I am capable of accomplishing things and that I am my own person" (Greg, 19).

"They really encourage me and usually always understand what is happening in my life. They really love me a lot!!!!" (Scott, 14).

"I just want to thank you, Mom and Dad, for loving me and for caring. In seeing something in me you don't see in my older brothers and younger brother, yet you encouraged me . . ." (Allen, 18).

I'm sure King Solomon would say "Amen" to all of the above. And he might suggest that Proverbs 15:23 bears repeating: ". . . how wonderful it is to be able to say the right thing at the right time!" (TLB).

FOR THOUGHT, DISCUSSION, AND ACTION

1. At your house, which is the truer statement—be honest.
   a. parents think they know it all
   b. teenagers think they know it all

What other barriers to good communication do you see between yourself and your child?

2. Which of the six Communication Killers discussed in chapter 5 are the biggest problems for you? Check at least three and rank them 1, 2, 3, in order of importance.

Gunslinger Words____   Discouraging Words____   Defensive Words____
Double Message Words____ Nagging Words____ Thoughtless Words____

Analyze just what causes you to use the kinds of words you checked. Is there a pattern or certain kind of timing involved?

3. Which of the following scriptural insights are most helpful to you in combating Communication Killers? Pick several and commit them to memory. Then—when the heat is on—try to remember them and live by them!

Proverbs 21:23: "Keep your mouth closed and you'll stay out of trouble" (TLB).

Proverbs 25:11: "A word aptly spoken is like apples of gold in settings of silver" (NIV).

Proverbs 10:19: "Don't talk so much. You keep putting your foot in your mouth. Be sensible and turn off the flow!" (TLB).

Proverbs 28:13: "A man who refuses to admit his mistakes can never be successful. But if he confesses and forsakes them, he gets another chance" (TLB).

Proverbs 17:9: "Love forgets mistakes. Nagging about them parts the best of friends" (TLB).

Proverbs 15:23: How wonderful to say the right thing at the right time" (TLB).

Romans 14:13: "Let us therefore stop turning critical eyes on one another. If we must be critical, let us be critical of our own conduct . . ." (Phillips).

6.

Do You Actually Listen?

"Listen to my opinion, on some things I am right" (**Jim, 18**).

THE SIX COMMUNICATION Killers described in chapter 5 are all armed and dangerous, but they are all minor league in comparison to Communication Enemy Number One: Not Listening. Christian psychoanalyst Paul Tournier says:

"It is impossible to overemphasize the immense need humans have to be really listened to. Listen to all the conversations of our world, between nations as well as those between couples. They are, for the most part, dialogues of the deaf." [1]

And it would be easy to add that you couldn't possibly overemphasize the immense need of teenagers to be really listened to. Among the hundreds of comments I collected from teenagers, close to half of them had something to do with lack of listening on at least two levels: (1) Their parents just tune them out; (2) If parents do try to listen, they don't listen for feelings—often because their own feelings are in the way.

"They're in Another World"

Again and again teenagers would complain about just not being able to get their parents' attention or interest:

"Sometimes they change the subject. Sometimes it goes in one ear and out the other. Sometimes they really listen to me" (Gary, 13).

"I'll be talking to my dad and the next minute he will have forgotten what I said because he was watching the TV or something" (Becky, 15).

"Mom—listen to me when I talk to you; you have a bad habit of ignoring me when I talk to you" (Kathy, 18).

"Sometimes when I want to talk with my mom she is too busy or in a hurry to go somewhere. And sometimes when she does listen it seems to pass right through her" (Nancy, 13).

"My parents never listen. My mom is kind of excused for it because she's ultrabusy, but my dad isn't. They just don't hear" (Roxanne, 14).

Examples of the preoccupied parent who seldom really listens to his children are legion. We would like to excuse this deadly habit by saying it is the pressure of modern-day life that forces our minds to wander and our ears to take the afternoon off. But the problem has been around for a long time. James wrote to first-century believers almost two thousand years ago and advised: "Everyone should be quick to listen . . ." (James 1:19, NIV). And almost one thousand years before that King Solomon penned these words of wisdom: "The wise man learns by listening . . ." (Prov. 21:11, TLB).

Listening—more precisely, the lack of it—has become such a problem that many large corporations are sending their executives and managers to classes to learn how to listen. Many teenagers wish their parents could attend also, including my own. In fact my entire family will tell you that "Dad is often off in his own little world." And it's true, being a writer, I take trips—mentally speaking—and I can wander far afield while others around me are talking. Any number of times I have made a comment or asked a question at the dinner table and received four exasperated looks along with the news that: "We just talked about that three minutes ago!"

So, I work at staying tuned in. I probably do better one on one, but I have to stay on my guard or I can go "wandering off" at any second.

"They Don't *Really* Listen"

Being tuned out is bad enough, but listening problems don't end there for teenagers and their parents. There is that little matter of feelings and opinions:

"Listen better and don't be so narrow-minded!" (Tammy, 19).

"I usually don't talk about anything real deep. I feel that if they didn't care before, why should they now?" (Suzie, 14).

"They only hear part of what you're saying so you have to repeat it, and then they don't fully understand what you are saying." (Jennie, 16).

"Try being a little less opinionated and a little more willing to listen" (Bob, 18).

"Listen to what teenagers say. They are not always right, but sometimes they have good ideas. Also, don't be afraid to admit you are wrong" (Craig, 19).

The above comments are illustrations of how we can try to tune in and then find we are listening for the wrong things. It's like being on two different wavelengths. All too often the parent is intent on getting the facts, while the teenager is really interested in communicating his feelings. This is often the reason for complaints about "being too opinionated."

For example, let's listen in on an imaginary—but all too typical—conversation between a teenager and his father:

Dad: How much will it cost? How far is it? What time will you get home?

Son: I dunno . . . quite a bit, but I think I've got enough, and if I need help, Tommy will loan me some. It's really going to be a *great* time—the biggest thing this year. *All* the kids are going. . . .

Dad: Well, that's nice, but *what time* are you getting in? And don't expect an advance on your allowance if you spend too much. I hope Tommy is willing to wait for his money. Fun is fine, but you've got to remember the bottom line.

Son: Okay, okay, we'll be back by 12 . . . I think. You don't have to make such a big deal out of it.

And so it goes. The teenager is primarily interested in the good time, the fun he'll have with the other kids. The father wants the facts—the bottom line. Mix the bottom-line thinking of the parents with the feeling-oriented messages of the teenager and indeed, in Tournier's terms, you have a "dialogue of the deaf," or at least the hard of hearing.

So what can be done? Doesn't a father have the right to know what time his teenager is getting in? Yes, he does. Should parents keep demanding that their teenager "grow up and start being more interested in the bottom line"? They can, but results will be minimal and frustration will probably rule the day. You don't have to give up your need to know the facts. After all, it is rather reasonable to want to know costs, distances, and estimated times of arrival home. But a better way to get that information is to listen for emotional signals *first*. Tune in and let your teenager know you really care about his feelings, and it will be much easier to get the facts and his cooperation.

The Art of Active Listening

Listening for feelings comes under several labels, depending on the psychologist or counseling method you deal with. Thomas Gordon, founder of Parent Effectiveness Training (P.E.T.) and author of a book by the same name, calls it "active listening." Haim Ginott, author of *Between Parent and Teenager,* calls it "acknowledging experience" or "reflecting feelings." Ross Campbell (*How to Really Love Your Teenager*) uses the term "focused attention."

Whatever you call it, the idea is to listen for the other person's feelings and then send back a message of empathic understanding. Empathy is putting yourself in the other person's shoes. You don't evaluate, offer advice, analyze or ask a lot of questions. You try to feed back a comment that lets the other person know you are trying to understand what he means and how he feels.

I prefer the term "active listening" because it suggests that you have to work at it. The process of active listening has two steps. First you must listen for the feeling; second, you feed back your message of empathy, which lets your teenager know you are trying to understand.

Let's look at some hypothetical examples:

Fourteen-year-old Peggy says she isn't walking to school anymore with Lisa. "She's a dud, a complete nurd." What is the feeling behind Peggy's remark? Anger and disgust are there and possibly hurt as well.

Let's try another one.

Sixteen-year-old Bobby says, "Just forget it. Leave me alone. You don't know what you're talking about." What are Bobby's feelings? Frustration and anger apply, and possibly there is a note of feeling alone and misunderstood.

Now try a couple of your own:

Thirteen-year-old Jerry says: "I can handle it. I don't need your help. Quit treating me like a little kid."

Fifteen-year-old Margie says: "I'd like to ask Jimmy to the Sadie Hawkins party, but what if he turns me down? I'd die!"

How did you do? Jerry is apparently feeling competent but a bit frustrated (not an uncommon condition for someone in junior high). Margie wants to do something but is afraid and unsure. Embarrassment lurks out there, ready to gobble her up.

Now let's go on to look at the difference between sending a message of empathy, rather than a Communication Killer. Let's go back to Peggy, who is not too happy with Lisa. Peggy said: "I'm through walking to school with Lisa. She's a dud . . . a complete nurd."

A typical Communication Killer many parents might send would be: "You shouldn't talk that way about your friends. How would you like to be called a nurd?"

To actively listen and reflect feelings without passing judgment, however, you might say: "Sounds like you and Lisa are on the outs . . ." That's about all you need to say—for openers. Let Peggy decide if she wants to tell you more. If she does, she might say: "You bet we are. I saw a note she wrote about me. She called me a lot worse than a nurd." To which you could reply: "It hurts when friends seem to turn against you. . . ."

And again, you wait for Peggy to offer more about the situation. The conversation might go on in any number of directions—perhaps to the point where Peggy might philosophically observe: "Oh well, Lisa has her moods. I'll call her in a few days and we'll make up." On the other hand, Peggy may only go so far with you, saying perhaps: "Yeah, well, I don't need *her*! I gotta do homework, I'll be in my room."

Reflecting feelings is not always easy—especially for a parent who wants to know every detail about the teenager's life. In this case it's the "real reason" behind the rift between Peggy and Lisa. It would be far easier to correct, to inquire, to pry, and to try to coax the facts out of your child, but all you do is succeed in killing communication rather than nurturing it.

What about 16-year-old Bob, who has just told his parents: "Just forget it. Leave me alone. You don't know what you're talking about." Bob is apparently feeling upset, misunderstood, frustrated, and a bit uptight. Any number of Communication Killers could put him in his place:

"Don't talk to us that way, young man. We're your parents, and you'll do what we say."

Or, "Why do you always have to be so difficult? We're only trying to help."

The first killer remark is the classic parent-in-command approach. The boy is being mouthy and needs to shape up. The second killer is a bit more subtle. It makes you look like you're trying to be reasonable, even helpful, but what you're really doing is putting Bob on the defensive, making him feel like the bad guy, and more misunderstood than ever.

So, how do you reflect feelings in this case? This time you are more directly involved and your parental authority (not to mention your dignity) has been slightly bruised. One possibility would be:

"You're pretty angry with us. You don't agree with our viewpoint. . . ." You could leave it there and maybe Bob would pick up on the opening you have given him by saying: "It's just that every time I want to do something it always seems like it's such a hassle."

To which you could reply: "You think we control you a little too much . . . that maybe we don't treat you like you're mature?"

"Yeah," Bob might reply. "A lot of guys my age have their driver's license, but I'm still riding my ten-speed."

If indeed the lack of the driver's license is the real issue then you have gotten somewhere. From there you may (or may not) work something out to resolve the conflict. There may be good reasons why Bob has to wait a few more weeks or months before he can get his license. But what's important here is that his parent would be willing to listen to how he feels. A college psych major I interviewed remembered a good point from his class notes when he told me: "If you recognize the kid's desires, whether you fulfill those desires or not, the kid will feel important. Whether the desires are met is not the point. The key is that they were considered and the child is considered as a person." (For more on conflict resolution techniques see chapter 9.)

They Don't Always Go by the Script

Whenever I talk about active listening, I always feel a word of caution is due. Active listening—listening for feelings and reflecting them back—is no magic wand. One of the problems I've always had with the "case study conversations" in Thomas Gordon's *Parent Effectiveness Training* or Haim Ginott's *Between Parent and Teenager* is that they always seem to go by the script.[2] The parents seem to say just the right thing and the teenager comes back with just the right response that keeps the conversation open and moving toward solution. Almost every case study ends happily with the child nicely resolving his own problem or at least being much more agreeable toward the parent. Frankly, my own children haven't always responded that way.

Often I try active listening and fail to reach first base. Or, if I do get to first, I get picked off before making it to second. Our kids are individuals and they don't always go by the "script." Of course, Drs. Gordon and Ginott can always tell me that I didn't send the right signal and that could very well be correct. Maybe I miss the signals, or completely misinterpret the feelings. Maybe I'm too angry to reflect feelings effectively or maybe I'm sending nonverbal vibes that completely blot out my attempts to communicate empathy. Gordon and Ginott don't stress the pitfalls of nonverbal communication. It's seldom just *what* we say; *how* we say it is always involved. If there is irritation, exasperation, or even honest weariness, it can kill communication on the spot. Active listening is a skill that I'm still learning. Sometimes I do fairly well; other times I blow it completely. The important thing, however, is that I keep trying. My attitude is set for trying to actively listen and reflect feelings rather than always firing back my own opinion (and often my own feelings which are sometimes hurt).

A basic premise from chapter 1 bears repeating here: Skills and standards are wonderful, but attitudes and commitment to the relationship are absolutely vital. If I at least try to leave an opening for my teenager to talk, communication may happen. I can't blast my way in.

Those Deafening Sounds of Silence

Right about here you could be one of those parents who is thinking, "I would like to try this active listening business, but there's nothing to listen to. My kid hasn't spoken over three or four words in six months and they are usually the same ones: 'When do we eat?' "

If you are one of the parents who copes with the sounds of silence, I understand. I have coped also, particularly with my sons, Jeff and Todd. My daughter, Kimberly, spoiled me, I guess. We could usually talk and still do. She is, in fact, still something of a counselor and encourager to me. One of the nicest serendipities I ever experienced occurred while Kim was still in high school. We had stopped for lunch in a restaurant and had been talking at a great rate. A young couple in their early 20s stopped at our table and he asked, "Is this your daughter?" I said, "Yes," and he replied, "It's easy to tell there's a lot of love between you."

Kim and I clicked in conversation, but with Jeff and Todd it was a different matter. Jeff and I spent a great portion of his high-school years working out hassles, groundings, girlfriends (he had at least eight, or was it ten?), etc., etc. But unless it was some kind of conflict or crisis, he had little to say because he "didn't feel comfortable" with me or his mother a lot of the time.

Currently, it's several years later and a whole new ball game. Now Jeff and I talk about everything—college courses, his plans for a career, his girlfriend. I didn't think it would ever happen, but it has. How it happened I'm still not sure. I think God had something to do with it, but that's the story I'm saving for a later chapter.

It's the spring of 1982 as I finish this book. Todd is 18 and counting the days until graduation from high school. I have not quite decided if Todd is especially silent or just believes in an economy of words. Whatever it is, he would never be accused of talking anyone to death—at least not around our house. I have tried everything: thoughtfulness, acceptance, respect, understanding, but to little avail. With Todd one thing works: waiting. When he is ready to talk, he talks, sometimes at length. I'd like to talk more, but whenever I push it, even ever so gently, the sounds of silence come crashing down.

All this does not sit well with my choleric-melancholy nature. At times I have engaged in pity parties that turn into depression. One day last winter I was reading Psalm 63 where David speaks of earnestly seeking God, so he can communicate, stay close, and be safe. Todd had been in a particularly silent mood and I was feeling rejected and defeated. So, I scribbled what I called: "A Father's Paraphrase of Psalm 63," which isn't really as much a paraphrase as it is a prayer:

"O Lord, O Lord, how lonely and hurt I feel because my son is so distant. How I thirst for one warm hello at the breakfast table, one intelligible answer to my inquiries about school, basketball, his pickup truck, his Doberman pup. How I long to find my son, who seems to wander in his own world, with his own kind, refusing to share with me his hurts, questions, problems. How I wish I could go into his room and just talk—warm, friendly, kidding, relaxed. Why is it so cold, stony, formal, and uptight? I ache, O Lord, will I always ache?''

As I said, that one came on one of my bad days. When I look at it now, I can hear the Lord saying, ''Yes, I know how you feel. Many of My children don't talk to Me much either. I just wait them out.''

Meanwhile my aches have diminished somewhat. In the last few months our conversations have picked up—a little. I have to admit his mother is more effective in chatting with Todd than I am. One of her frequent practices is to go into his room just after he has hit the sack and rub either his back or his feet, which are often sore from playing basketball, working all day, etc. As Mom rubs, they often share feelings or just ''how did the day go?'' talk. You might call it ''communication by fingertips.'' As I mentioned, Todd talks, but on his terms.

As I interviewed other teenagers on the ''silence syndrome'' I got further insights on why they clam up:

Amy, a 15-year-old high-schooler, wanted her parents to know: ''Sometimes kids just can't share a problem with their parents, they have to battle it out themselves. You can't pressure them to know everything . . . I still love you.''

Shirley, 16, and in the same youth group as Amy, said of her parents: ''I love them lots and I don't ever want to have them think I don't because I don't talk to them about everything all the time.''

Heidi, 15, revealed: ''I'm quieter than my sisters and keep feelings and emotions inside (telling them I love them, etc.). It's hard for me to say what I'm thinking, and some topics I can't talk freely about to them. I like to keep things to myself.''

Clea, a junior in college, remembers how her silent times in high school would backfire on her:

''I would come home . . . it was mostly when I had been away for a weekend, or for camp or something. I'd come home and get,

'How was it and who was there? And what did you do, and who spoke?' And I'm just going, 'Don't . . . I just want to sit here. I don't want to talk. I've been talking all week, all weekend. I don't want to tell you anything right now. I just want to be by myself.' So then they would shut up and wouldn't say anything. Later, I'd start feeling at home again and I'd start thinking about how it was and I'd want to talk. And I'd say, 'Oh, you know what happened, Mom—at camp?' But she'd be off somewhere else, and then I couldn't talk to her . . . that was always a conflict.''

I get several messages from the above comments. One is that there are many stumbling blocks to communication and teenagers sometimes have their reasons for being silent that have nothing to do with how they feel about their parents. Another message is that they do want to communicate, but on their own terms. One of the questions on the Norman/Harris poll of 160,000 teenagers asked: "Can you tell either or both of your parents how you think you feel about most things?" Eighty-three percent replied: "Yes, usually, sometimes."[3]

A third message is that when communicating with teenagers, it's all a matter of timing. There is a time to talk, a time to listen, a time to wait, and wait, and wait. . . .

Key Attitude #6: Perseverance

"How well do I listen?" is a major question for any parent who takes Ephesians 6:4 seriously. As Paul said, ". . . do not exasperate your children . . ." (NIV). Nothing seems to exasperate teenagers like not being heard. And when parents don't hear them, they quickly translate it into not caring about their feelings, which are always very close to the surface.

The attitude for every parent who wants to become a better listener is *perseverance*. Patience certainly fits here, too, but perseverance is better. To learn to really listen takes a determined, stick-it-out kind of patience. Perseverance is patience with teeth in it.

Perseverance is needed in large doses to fight the two levels of nonlistening that go on in many homes. One level is that of tuning out the other party; this happens when we are too preoccupied with our own problems. We have already heard from several young people on that, but comments by Char, a college freshman, are especially poignant:

"My parents, I can't communicate with them. They don't listen to me. They don't listen to me when they're off in their own little world. Like I'm trying to say something to my dad and he'll say, 'Uh-huh, but go get me a glass of milk, please.' I think, 'I'm not your slave, Dad.' I have to say, 'Will you just sit down and *listen* to me?' He goes, 'I have been listening to you.' And I say, 'No, you haven't.' When the TV's on and everything, I have to turn it off and make him sit down and then I talk to him. And my mom, if she's in a bad mood, I have to say, 'Now, just start listening to me a little bit. Get out of your little pity party.' That doesn't happen all the time, but sometimes that's why she can't listen to me. I do it, too. I can get all 'poor little me,' but then I can't understand anybody else's problems."

Char is only 18, but she already has a good handle on life. To be able to listen and understand somebody else's problems is the key to avoiding that second all-important level of nonlistening—failing to hear how people really feel inside.

Kim, a 16-year-old high school junior, put it this way as she and some of her friends talked with me one afternoon in a pizza parlor:

"Well, they (parents) have different lives. My mom will come home and she'll talk about her job and that's all that interests her. She doesn't really ask, 'Well, how was your day?' or anything like that. And then when I do talk to her, she tries to understand, but she tries to tell me what to do, and I don't think I need advice, I think I just need understanding."

Understanding—seems like we've heard that word before. There are two ways to respond to what Kim and Char said. One is to sigh or bristle and wonder why teenagers can't grow up a little and understand their parents for a change. If only they knew what it was like to worry about the bills, to get up and go to work every day, etc., etc. And there's a lot of truth to that. It would be nice to have your teenager put his arm around you and say, "Sounds like you had a rough day . . . tell me about it." It would be nice, but it probably won't happen for awhile yet. As Ross Campbell reminds us, teenagers are children in large bodies, not mature adults.[4]

The other way to react is to ask God for more strength to listen actively, compassionately, understandingly. As I prepared a study guide for use with some parents in a session on active listening, I penciled in the phrase, "actively listen." My wife, Jackie, kindly serves as my expert typist, and as she typed that particular line she misread my somewhat suspect handwriting to say: "*actually* listen."

When I saw the "mistake" I decided it wasn't really a mistake at all. To *actually listen* is the name of the game. You can't reflect feelings unless you actually listen. You can't communicate unless you actually listen. Keep at it and some day you may hear your teenager say, "My folks are really trying. The other day they actually listened to me!"

FOR THOUGHT, DISCUSSION, AND ACTION

1. On a scale of 1 to 10 (10 being excellent), how would you rate yourself as a listener? Do you listen for facts only, or do you also consciously try to filter out the feelings?

2. Some parents think to "actively listen" means to listen carefully so they can give some "good advice." But when you actively listen, you listen for feelings and try to send back a message of empathy rather than advice or judgment. Don't wait for some tense or sticky situation to practice active listening. Try it when things are going well. For example, your teenager comes in obviously feeling good. Try saying, "Sounds like you had a good day . . ." and see where it goes from there.

3. Be sure you know the difference between reflecting a feeling and just parroting what your teenager says. To review some of the examples in this chapter:

Sixteen-year-old Bobby says: "Just forget it. Leave me alone."

Parroting: "You want us to forget it and leave you alone. . . ."

Reflecting feelings (active listening): "Sounds like you feel that we don't understand your problem. . . ."

Fifteen-year-old Margie says: "I'd like to ask Jimmy to the Sadie Hawkins party, but what if he turns me down? I'd die!"

Parroting: You want to ask Jimmy to the party, but if he turns you down, you'll die. . . ."

Reflecting feelings (active listening): "It would be really embarrassing to get turned down, wouldn't it?"

4. Be wary of nonverbal communication. Your tone of voice, your stance, the look on your face can all belie your attempts to actively listen in a genuine way.

7.

Anger—The Enemy Within

"I yell, or I just stand there and escape inside myself" **(Jennie, 16).**

HOW BIG A PART does anger play in communication problems with your teenager?

Don't answer too quickly. Think about it for a minute. As the last two chapters show, whenever Communication Killers attack, anger often leads the charge. Gunslinger Words sting to cause anger. Defensive Words are fired back in more anger. Nagging Words raise hackles, and nothing is more exasperating than not being listened to.

In almost every family anger is the mortal enemy lurking within. Sometimes it erupts; sometimes it smolders, but it is there. David Mace, one of the leading marriage and family specialists in the world, has spent almost fifty years working for better marriages and happier families in sixty-one countries. He observes:

1. When a marriage ends in divorce, or a family breaks down, the failure always takes place from the inside.

2. The generally supposed causes of marital trouble—difficulties with sex, money, in-laws, and child raising—are *not the real causes.* These are only the *arenas* in which the inner failure of the relationship is outwardly demonstrated.

3. The inner failure of a close relationship takes place for the same reason—*because the persons involved have been unable to achieve mutual love and intimacy.*

4. The failure to achieve love and intimacy is almost always due to *the inability of the persons concerned to deal creatively with anger.*[1]

Mace goes on to make two more statements that have tremendous implications for parents and their children:

1. Marriage and family living generates, in normal people, more anger than they experience in any other social situation in which they habitually find themselves.
2. The overwhelming majority of family members know of only two ways of dealing with anger—to vent it, or to suppress it. Both of these methods are destructive of love and intimacy.[2]

Dr. Mace's claims might startle some people. Others might say he's absolutely right, including most policemen who have to answer the call they dread: family disturbance. But after fifty years of helping families, and rearing one of his own, Dr. Mace is so convinced of his premise that he has written a helpful book on how to deal effectively with anger in the family—*Love and Anger in Marriage.*[3]

The Anger Is There

Fifteen-year-old Michelle and her father are a vivid example of the anger merry-go-round in the family:

"Well, my dad, he gets mad real easy. And when he's mad and stuff he doesn't want to talk about it, you know. And I say, 'Dad, I want to talk about it.' And he'll say, 'No, we'll talk about it when I want to talk about it.' And I say, 'Dad, I want to talk about it *now!*' And I get mad because he just tries to put me off. And I yell at him, and I scream at him, and then I say all this really bad stuff to him. I want to hurt him because he hurts me. Then I just go in my room and sit there, and sometimes he comes in and wants to talk and by then I don't want to. Then, when he doesn't want to, I want him to talk. It's kind of like, we have a gap, you know?"

Jane, a college junior, remembers a lot of tension with her mother during high-school years.

''It was hard for me to realize that my mom was interested in me and not that she was being nosy and trying to irritate me. A lot of times we had big blowups where I would just say, 'Get off my back!' It wasn't that I was mad at her or anything but just that I needed my space.''

John,[4] a college freshman, felt a lot of anger toward his mother during high school, but for another reason. A quiet loner, John had two talkative brothers who communicated readily with their mother, while he could not. He recalls:

''I just never felt I could really come to her with anything, and when I did, I felt that she would listen for a minute and then it was gone. On the other hand, it really irritated me whenever I saw her talking to my older and younger brothers. Just the way she'd look at them when she talked, I could tell that she was really intently listening. And it really irritated me cause a lot of times I would feel she wasn't listening to me.''

Kari, 17, has a father who is in law enforcement. She says:

''My dad gets really mad really easy. Like if you spill something at dinner, he blows up. Or, like you say something and he takes it the wrong way and starts yelling and everything. He's really impatient. I think part of that is probably because of his job . . . all day long people are hassling him and calling him names and that sort of thing.''

Just What Is Anger?

Anger comes from many directions, for many reasons. Michelle and her father used alternating blowups and silence to get at each other. Jane ''wasn't mad or anything,'' but she had blowups with her mother because she ''needed space.'' John used the word ''irritated'' twice as he described his mother listening intently to his brothers, but practically ignoring him.

What is anger anyway? The dictionary will tell you it comes

from a Latin root word that means "to strangle" and that it means: "A strong feeling excited by a real or supposed injury; often accompanied by a desire to take vengeance or to obtain satisfaction from the offending party; resentment; wrath; ire."[5]

Keep that definition in mind; we'll be coming back to it—especially the part about the desire for vengeance. Anger goes by a lot of names: displeasure, hostility, indignation, exasperation are just a few. Another name for most kinds of anger could be "destruction." Anger tears apart marriages and parent-child relationships. Worst of all, it destroys the persons who are giving or receiving it. Anger is truly "the enemy within."

What Causes Anger?

There are at least three major causes of anger: fear, hurt, and frustration.[6]

Anger caused by fear is a natural response when we feel threatened and in danger. Fear is often behind a parent's anger toward a teenager who gets in late, who doesn't call to let everyone know he's safe, etc. Parental fear for a teenager's safety is always a point of contention. The parents are angry because the teenager is inconsiderate enough to put them through all that fear and worry.

Much of the anger Jackie and I felt toward Jeff when he came in late was motivated by fear for his safety. The crowning event took place in his junior year after his basketball team had absorbed a one point loss. It was a Friday night so we didn't expect him until 12:30 or 1:00 A.M. (I can't recall the exact curfew we had him on then.) The clock ticked on and at 2:00 he still wasn't home. By 2:45 I started making some phone calls: the hospital, the Highway Patrol, and the Sheriff's office. At 3:00 A.M., just as a Sheriff's deputy had left the phone to go check for any newly occupied cells, Jeff walked in. He explained that he had been sitting parked, alone, down by the wash, mulling over the agony of defeat, and he had fallen asleep.

Fear causes anger in teenagers, too, but they are not as apt to describe it in those words. Michelle and Kari, two girls who are quoted in the opening part of this chapter, would get angry with their fathers after the fathers ''blew up'' at them. These encounters caused them to be afraid, but they responded by lashing back, a natural way to cope with fearful and anxious feelings.

Anger caused by hurt, particularly hurt feelings, makes us want to strike back to protect our dignity and pride. A mother attending one of my parents' classes reported that her 13-year-old daughter was failing to do chores, doing poor school work, and showing disrespect and rebellion in general. The mother admitted to anger and hurt feelings because her daughter's actions threatened her parental authority and caused her to feel insecure.

I related to what she was saying, because hurt feelings have always been a key cause of my anger toward my own kids. There have been those times when they don't talk, times when they act like they don't care, and times when they seem to value me only as a built-in branch of the local bank. My feelings get hurt and I think, ''How can they do this to me, such a nice guy, such a loving father? Move over Rodney Dangerfield. You aren't the only one who 'don't get no respect!' ''

Of course, teenagers get angry over hurt feelings, too. John, the shy, retiring young man described earlier, got his feelings hurt when his mother communicated so much better with his talkative, outgoing brothers. He would get angry when his mother seemed to almost ignore his attempts to communicate. This went on until his senior year in high school, when he decided to come out of his shell and be more talkative to everyone in general. As soon as that happened communication with his mother improved. ''I'm not as silent anymore,'' says John, ''and the (communication) gap is kind of broken.''

Anger caused by frustration is probably the most prevalent perpetrator of family strife. To be frustrated is to be unable to get what you want. You have a goal or a desire and your path is blocked. Teenagers I surveyed, as well as parents' groups I worked with, felt plenty of frustration.

I asked one group of young people: "Why do people in families get angry?" Fifty percent listed frustration as the chief cause. Specific examples of frustration and anger that students listed included these comments:

"My father sometimes makes promises he doesn't or can't keep" (Christi, 18).

"When watching a TV show, they don't even realize you're there watching it, and they change the channel even after I've said, 'I was watching that' " (Eugene, 16).

"(My parents) nag, don't come through on promises, judge my friends" (Jennifer, 16).

"LECTURES!" (Pam, 13).

"Tell me to go to bed in the middle of a TV program" (Bill, 13).

"They ask me to do something when I'm tired, or they just talk to me about their problems when I wish not to hear them" (Steve, 15).

When I talked with one parents' class about anger, they had their own list of frustrations caused by their children. "Failing to do chores and other responsibilities" came up more than any other answer. Other frequently mentioned problems were "using abusive or impertinent language," "giving me the silent treatment," and "poor schoolwork."

One mother mentioned "incessant arguing," another listed. "listening to loud rock music."

Another mother of five, whose children's ages range from 15 years down to 7 months, listed her chief frustration as: "They do things they *know* they aren't supposed to do."

A father, who also has five children, was frustrated because "They fail to do the request in a timely order," and he wondered , "How do I get my concept onto their level?"

Dr. David Mace's comments about anger seem to echo more loudly than ever. Living in an intimate situation such as the family unit is bound to cause frustration, irritation, and anger. A college junior said it quite well when he told me: "It's hard to live in a close bond like a family structure and not get rubbed the wrong way by others. If only we could all learn to take a little more."

And *give* a little more, too.

Who Really Makes You Angry?

The next time you feel angry try finding the cause for your anger in the answers to three questions:

Am I afraid of someone or something?

Do I feel hurt, especially my feelings?

Am I being frustrated—not able to get or do what I want to do?

By asking these questions you are seeking the cause for your anger *within yourself.* You are not blaming it on someone or something else. All of us have said something like this: "He makes me so mad!" or "This car has bugged me for the last time—to the junk yard!"

It is quite common—and easy—to want to blame our anger on someone or something, but psychologists have identified certain parts of the brain as the real trigger for our angry responses. Psychotherapist Archibald Hart writes: "The ideas, thoughts and perceptions we experience and our interpretations of these events trigger our angry response."[7] What other people—our teenagers for example—do or say is not what makes us angry. It is what we *think* about what is done or said that makes us angry. In short, people and events don't make us angry; *we make ourselves angry.*

There are three basic ways to handle anger:

1. You can let it out.
2. You can keep it in.
3. You can control it.

Let's look at each of them.

A Fool Gives Vent to His Anger

The most well-known method for handling anger is the worst: "letting it all hang out" or "blowing up." Some psychologists believe that blowing up or "venting" is a healthy way to handle anger because you get it off your chest, and you are not subject to the dangers of repression, trying to ignore anger while it eats you alive. Other psychologists, including Archibald Hart, question the use of venting. Hart writes:

"I have worked in therapy with enough angry people to know that while helping them to get angry more frequently and encouraging them to express it more openly may be emotionally satisfying, it neither removes the cause for the anger nor drains away the angry feelings at all times. Above all else, this approach does not help people to come to terms with their frustration proneness nor teach them how to heal their hurts."[8]

For the parent of teenagers, venting has to be a questionable approach to handling anger. Emotionally the teenager is more child than adult, and he usually doesn't know how to handle his own anger, much less yours.

Many of the teenagers I surveyed described their parents' anger in terms of blowing up or ventilating:

"It seems like most of the time they blow up and shout" (Carrie, 15).

"My mom will spank or scream . . ." (Chris, 14).

"They ground me. They shout or hit and give lectures" (Andrea, 13).

"My mom yells and says that she thought I was such a great Christian . . ." (Becky, 15).

Shouting, screaming, lecturing, spanking, hitting—all are familiar words when describing family strife. Often there is an uproar; at other times it's possible to speak quietly but still use bitter, biting language that cuts and hurts. Solomon had ventilating in mind when he wrote: "A fool gives full vent to his anger, but a wise man keeps himself under control" (Prov. 29:11, NIV).

Angry? Who? Me?

Instead of letting anger out, you can hold it in. There are healthy and unhealthy ways to do this.

Repression is an unhealthy way of holding anger in. To repress anger is to refuse to admit that you are angry. This often happens in Christian families where people have been taught that "anger is a sin." Anger is an emotion that we all must deal with, but it is not necessarily a sin. Paul advised the Ephesian Christians to "be . . . angry, and sin not" (Eph. 4:26, KJV). What is sinful is to try to keep anger bottled up inside and refuse to admit that it is there. Repressed anger often ruins relationships and communication by coming out in the form of mild irritation or constant criticism. Or, repressed anger can turn on the person who is holding it in and cause anything from ulcers to migraine headaches.

Clea remembers how her father repressed his anger when she was a teenager in high school:

"My dad and I are very much alike. We're very stubborn, and when we tried to work out a problem between us, we couldn't and my dad would walk off and my mom would say, 'Go talk to him.' And I would and I'd say, 'Dad, you're mad.' And he'd say, 'No, I'm not mad.' And he would just totally deny . . . he wouldn't talk . . . nothing."

Suppression is a more positive way to hold anger in. Probably the most familiar way people suppress anger is to "count to ten" or do some equivalent thing to get themselves under control. They know they are angry and they are consciously trying to keep it in check instead of dumping all over everyone. John, the college freshman who couldn't communicate as well with his mother as his brothers did, explains how he tries to suppress his anger:

". . . it's just a lot of little things that make me angry . . . and they start building up inside me, but I don't want to blow because then I feel I'm going to hurt the person who made me angry. So they just build up inside me, and I hurt myself a lot more than I should. Instead of talking to that person, I'll go talk to somebody else who will just sit there and listen to me, which relieves the small irritations."

As Solomon put it, "A wise man controls his temper. He knows that anger causes mistakes" (Prov. 14:29, TLB). Suppressing anger is a good start on controlling it, but in many instances, particularly in a family, you need to go beyond suppression to find a positive way to deal with what is causing the anger in the first place.

There are many excellent systems for coping with anger, but I believe that parents with teenagers need to develop two strengths above all others:

1. They must learn to deal with frustration.
2. They must learn to forgive.

Does it sound too simple? Perhaps, but experience with my own teenagers, and what I hear hundreds of others saying, tells me otherwise. Unlocking the secrets of frustration and forgiveness are absolutely basic to controlling anger in the family.

How Frustration Becomes a Frankenstein

An earlier section of this chapter described *frustration* as probably the major cause of anger in many homes. We get frustrated when we don't get what we want. In this simple definition is a clue to what we can do about frustration.

One helpful thing is to understand just how frustration escalates into full-blown anger. The more we think about what is frustrating us, the more angry we become. Psychotherapist Paul Hauck tells his patients: "If you did not think angry thoughts, you could not become angry." He believes we go through a six-step process as we think ourselves into being angry:[9]

1. "I want something." (No problem yet, everyone has desires. It is part of being alive.)

2. "I didn't get what I wanted and I'm frustrated." (We all know what it is like not to have our desires realized.)

3. "It is awful and terrible not to get what I want." (At this point whatever frustrated you is becoming a catastrophe of sorts. You are starting to get bothered.)

4. "You shouldn't frustrate me! I must have my way." (At this point you are asking for anger. You are demanding that your desire be granted.)

5. "You're bad for frustrating me." (Now you start thinking about revenge or lashing back. It is at this point that you prepare to

fire on whomever or whatever is frustrating you. It may be verbal, it may be a blow, it may be worse.)

6. "Bad people ought to be punished." (Anger has taken you over the edge. You have gotten revenge, or at least tried to. In many instances this may mean anything from a sarcastic retort to a shouted obscenity. In other cases it can mean a left hook, a right cross, or squeezing a trigger. As James put it, ". . . sin, when it is full-grown, gives birth to death" (James 1:15, NIV).

Whether we want to admit it or not, that is the sequence we go through as we allow frustration to drive us up the wall. Sometimes these six steps take only a few seconds; in other cases it can take a half hour, a day, or several weeks, or even years to complete the six-step process.

Knowing the six-step sequence is helpful, but what can we do to halt the process in midfrustration? When starting to feel frustrated with your teenager, you can head off anger with some basic questions:

1. I did not get what I wanted from my teenager, but how badly do I need it? What difference will it make if I don't get it?

2. I did not get my way with my teenager in this case, but is it really serious? What is at stake here? His self-esteem? My pride? Allowing him to "get away with irresponsibility"?

3. My teenager has just gotten into another scrape with the neighbors (or his sister, or his teacher, etc., etc.). This is frustrating, but do I have to get disturbed? Is it the end of the world?

4. My teenager has refused to eat, been late for supper, is out past curfew, etc. etc. Is this a catastrophe or an annoyance? If it is really more in the annoyance category, is it necessary for me to think it is "awful"?

It's fairly obvious that these questions are designed to help you, the parent, keep your cool. But, you may be saying, "Wait a minute, in *this* case I *do* need it. It *is* serious. A lot *is* at stake. This *is* more than just annoying."

Okay, I hear you. I've had plenty of instances with my teenagers where I would be right in there with you. BUT, there have been plenty of other instances where I got frustrated, and then angry (the six steps), *but I didn't have to.* I could have asked myself any one of those questions above and cut my frustration off at ground level before it grew up into a thorny angry thistle that stung me and my teenagers.

Those four clusters of questions are no sure-fire cure for frustration and anger. *There is no sure-fire cure.* I still face many frustrating situations, but if I have the six-step process in mind, I can see what is happening. I can stop and ask myself some questions that might just turn the whole situation around. If nothing else, using these "frustration control" methods can keep me from doing or saying things I will regret, probably sooner than later.

Teenagers live life with a certain reckless abandon, with little thought for anyone but themselves and their immediate plans (the next five minutes). Yesterday is ancient history; tomorrow is the distant future, next week sounds like the twenty-fifth century. Parents can let all this frustrate them, or they can "fight back" by not fighting back. In other words, simply accept what is there. The behavior of your teenager may not be what you like or approve, but it does no good to let it get to you.

Forgive Seventy Times What?

Remember that dictionary definition of anger earlier in this chapter? "A strong feeling excited by a real or supposed injury; often accompanied by a desire to take vengeance or to obtain satisfaction from the offending party." Anger brings a desire for revenge. The best way to cope with anger (and frustration as well) is to forgive. Before you dismiss this as too simplistic, ask yourself: "What is forgiveness?" I like Archibald Hart's definition: "Forgiveness is surrendering my right to hurt you back if you hurt me."[10]

You might argue that nobody really has the *right* to hurt somebody back, but there is no question that we often have the *desire*. What is there about living in the intimate atmosphere of a family that makes that desire to "hurt back" extra strong? Our sense of justice says, "Even the score . . . don't let him get away with that . . . put her in her place . . ." and on and on. As parents we like to excuse our vengeance-taking under the guise of "discipline" or "Christian training," but nobody is really fooled. At the heart of it all is anger and a lack of forgiveness.

Peter had a rather well-known conversation with Jesus about forgiveness. He asked the Lord how many times he should forgive his brother when his brother did him wrong. Seven times? Peter thought Jesus would put a big star by his name for that one. The rabbis of the day taught that forgiving someone three times was plenty. Peter had doubled that and added one for good measure. But Jesus had news for him: "No, not seven times, . . . but seventy times seven" (Matt. 18:22, TEV).

Did Jesus mean that the new standard was 490? No, He used one of His favorite teaching methods: exaggerating to make a point. He meant that true forgiveness is unlimited. You do it over and over and over. Forgiving is not to be a special or unusual event; *it is a way of life.* How true this is in the family and what a perfect strategy for combating frustration and anger.

Without forgiveness the minor annoyance of frustration quickly grows into a catastrophe and we immediately start to play the well-known game: "Ain't it awful!" More precisely, we look at our teenagers and say, "Ain't he (or she) awful!" Without forgiveness, frustration flares into anger that can blaze and explode and exact a terrible price. Or it can smolder in the form of resentment, only to flare up again in more flames and more explosions.

The Battle at Kitchen Sink

I know whereof I speak. Frustration and anger ate at me until the night we had the closest thing to Mt. St. Helens ever endured in the Ridenour household. For several weeks tension had been growing between Jeff and me. It was a warm spring evening, a few weeks before Jeff was to graduate from high school. All I was wearing was a pair of cut offs and jogging shoes. I found Jeff in the kitchen doing, of all things, the dishes by himself.

It seems ironic now, but instead of being impressed with Jeff's strange new devotion to household duties, I started quizzing him on something that he had been doing, or not doing, that irritated me. Neither one of us can recall now what it was, but we do remember that the conversation quickly escalated.

He snarled something back at my initial inquiry, I sharply repeated my question. He snarled some more. My voice rose and I started across the kitchen, saying something like, "I'm fed up with your smart mouth!"

Jeff wouldn't look at me. He just kept washing a pot and muttering about being "sick of this!"

"I want you to look at me when I'm talking to you—do you understand me!" I almost shouted.

I grabbed Jeff's arm, spun him around, and glared into blazing eyes that glared right back. Actually he glared down a bit. He is 6-foot-4, I am 6-foot-2. I outweighed him by at least forty pounds, and he sensed that I was angry enough to do more than talk. So, being 18 and pretty angry himself, he said: "Oh, now the big Christian father is gonna beat up his son, huh?"

At this point "big Christian father" was boiling mad. All the frustration—the missed curfews, the hassles, the bitter exchanges—turned a normally patient, seldom really loud, and never violent Christian father into a raging bull.

"You treat me like . . . !" I shouted, my face about six inches from Jeff's. "Don't you tempt me!"

Jeff put his hands behind his back and cocked his chin in the air another inch or two. "C'mon, hit me. C'mon, big Christian man, hit me!"

So I did. It wasn't much of a punch, more of a left hook slap in the mouth.

"Did it feel good?" Jeff wanted to know. "Hit me again, Christian man."

I hit him again, another open left hand to his cheek. I really don't know if I would have followed up with heavier artillery. At that moment I finally became aware of a certain amount of pressure and pain on my bare arms. It was my wife, Jackie, trying to pull me off. She had been upstairs and our other two children, Kim and Todd, had heard the uproar. Frightened, they had dashed in pleading, "Mom, go stop him!"

As Jackie rushed into the kitchen, she saw me holding Jeff "halfway off the floor by the shirt." The look on his face was a mixture of anger, terror, and defiance. She grabbed me and tried to pull me off, but I never even noticed. To get my attention she started raking her fingernails up and down my arms, saying, "Honey, stop it! Go get control of yourself! This is ridiculous!"

Actually the whole thing was a bit beyond ridiculous, but being a proper Melancholy, she described it with precise constraint.

Big Christian father, alias Raging Bull, spun around to face the new matador that was goading him. Jackie is 5-foot-6, 118 pounds. In thirty years of marriage I have never struck her. At that moment, however, I was "firm." I grabbed her by both arms and marched her backwards out of the kitchen, through the hall and to the stairs.

"Get upstairs!" I bellowed. "I am running this house!"

As Jackie scampered to a safer perch several steps out of my reach, I whirled and bolted out of the front door, running down the street, around the corner and down the hill to the nearby school-yard that had served as my jogging track for many years. Hot tears of rage mixed with remorse poured down my face as I tried to tell God how I felt. About all that came out was, "Lord, I blew it, I really blew it. I'm a failure, an idiot, I really blew it. What am I gonna do now? Help me!"

There's a verse in Romans chapter 8 that talks about the Spirit helping us in our weakness when we don't know how to pray. He intercedes for us with groans that words cannot express.[11] I trust that verse was at work as I ran around the field; I was doing plenty of my own groaning and the Spirit was interceding.

I'm not sure how far I ran, maybe a mile or two. As I cooled down, depression started to set in. I walked slowly up the hill and back to the house. I was totally dejected. Some people might smile and say, "So what's the big deal? The kid got smart and you slapped him a couple of times—he had it coming." But for me far more had happened than that. In my entire adult life I had never hit another person. Now I had clobbered my son, terrorized my family, and made a complete fool of myself.

I wish I could tell you I went home, apologized to Jeff, and that we fell into each other's arms in a warm prayer of reconciliation. But that's not what happened. To be honest, I'm not sure of the details. It wasn't a case of being too proud to say I was sorry. I have often apologized to my children. But this was different. Jackie remembers I told her I was sorry and that I went into Jeff's room and apologized to him, but he hardly acknowledged me. He was nursing his wounded spirit.

He tells me now that after I had bolted out the door he had gone upstairs to his room. He was hurting inside and wanted to cry, but "no way" was he going to cry in front of me. Kim came into his room and started to talk and then he broke down. "Kim, I'm getting out of here right after I graduate," Jeff had sobbed bitterly. Jeff didn't get out right after graduation. He stuck around another year before moving out. And when he did, that was also a traumatic event, especially for Jackie, but that's another story I'll save for later.

Jeff remembers that it was "pretty tense between us" for the next few weeks, that I "didn't enjoy talking much." That's probably true. I was working the whole thing through. Anger had invaded my life and my family in a new and violent way. A chord deep within me had been struck, and when the final reverberations died away my attitude was different.

I doubt that I could say I was a "brand new father," but I certainly had undergone an overhaul. At that time I had never heard of Paul Hauck's six-step process from frustration to angry enough to lash out. I had not yet read Archibald Hart's thoughts on anger and forgiveness. God did a slow but steady work within me (it seems I seldom let Him work very fast), and I realized that the "answer" to my tension with Jeff was to forgive. From that time on the hassles were fewer and much less intense. I would still get frustrated and angry, but instead of allowing it to corrode and eat at me I would ask myself questions like: "I'm not getting my way, but how important is this, really? Can I find a way to survive?"

It was not a case of Jeff taking over the house, far from it. He had engaged Raging Bull once and wasn't too interested in a rematch. But from that chaotic night on I changed. I learned that frustration and anger are really not worth their inflated price. I learned a little something about forgiveness.

Key Attitude #7: Forgiveness

My battle at the kitchen sink with Jeff convinced me that David Mace is right when he says anger is the real enemy in the family. The hassles, the arguments, the bad scenes are only the arenas where we act out our failure to control frustration and anger. Every chapter in this book emphasizes an "attitude" that parents should develop, but *forgiveness* is the key attitude of all.

Without forgiveness there can be little understanding, respect, letting go, acceptance, thoughtfulness, and patient perseverance. Forgiveness is the oil that allows parent and child to rub together in harmony, instead of grating and grinding on each other. Forgiveness is what opens communication channels and keeps them open.

Forgiveness is not giving up and copping out in permissive disgust. We'll get into that in the next three chapters, which deal with authority and discipline.

Forgiveness is not forgetting. Archibald Hart labels the cliché, "Forgive and forget," as trite and simplistic, and I agree. I cannot "forget" the hurts, the slights, the frustrations. Hart writes: "The solution lies not in forgetting—but in breaking the power of your memories to re-create the feelings of hurt."[12]

And how do I break the power of those memories? By remembering that God first forgave me. I am not much for simple solutions to complex problems. I see the gray much more than the clear black and white. *But some things are simply true,* and we must use them as foundations to work out all our "Yes, buts," "What abouts," and "How do I's" as best we can. And this is a true saying: In Christ, God has forgiven me, and only as I forgive can I know His peace and power.

FOR THOUGHT, DISCUSSION, AND ACTION

1. Read Jesus' parable of the unmerciful servant in Matthew 18:23–35. Then compare the characters in the parable to your relationship with your teenager. Are there times when you take the role of the forgiven, but unmerciful, servant who owed the king millions while your teenager is the other servant who owes you ten dollars? We often separate "spiritual things" from practical, everyday problems. Can being forgiven by God really affect how we treat our children? Is this a good parable to keep in mind next time your teenager frustrates you or makes you angry?

2. Do you agree that people or things don't make you angry, but that you make yourself angry? What are some basic questions to ask yourself when you feel anger coming on?

3. Is it possible to be angry and sin not? Read Ephesians 4:26–32. Pick one or more of Paul's suggestions for controlling anger and make a deliberate effort to practice it.

4. Handling anger in yourself is your first responsibility, but what about handling anger in others—especially your teenager? Here are some tips:[13]

   . . . Expect it. Many teenagers get angry frequently. Instead of wringing your hands over such "unchristian behavior" realize it is one method teenagers use to separate from their parents and become individuals.

   . . . When your teenager gets angry, be sure to identify the problem. Many times it is the teenager's problem and you are not involved. Realizing it is not your problem will help keep you from getting sucked into an angry exchange. (Note: in other instances the problem belongs to both of you and your relationship is involved. Then you need to work it out together. See chapter 9.)

   . . . Try to get at the real reason behind your teenager's anger. Is he afraid, hurt, frustrated? Ask him what he would be feeling if he did not feel anger.

. . . Listen for feelings and try to show empathy. Reflect your teenager's feelings back to him without passing judgment, giving advice, or trying to make him feel guilty. (Review chapter 6 on active listening.)

. . . Don't be a garbage dump. It does no one any good if you just take continued abuse with a smile. If you are hurt or provoked, forgive your teenager, not with a formal ceremony, but simply by refusing to try to hurt or provoke in return. Send an ''I'' message to let your teenager know that his anger is not acceptable and that you want to work it out. (For more on ''I'' messages and resolving conflict, see chapter 9.)

Unit III: Authority

Using Authority with Teenagers—
A Little Goes a Long Way

The third message sent by teenagers interviewed for this book centers around the use of parental authority. Rules, discipline, trust, fairness are all involved. It's a tough area, often about as safe as a mine field. In the next three chapters we'll take a look at:

. . . parenting styles—authoritarian, permissive, authoritative.

. . . why authoritarian and permissive parenting don't work.

. . . authoritative parenting—Ephesians 6:4 in action.

. . . the fine art of resolving conflicts.

. . . how to try to work it so everybody wins.

. . . what to do when somebody has to lose.

. . . the key attitudes of self-control, fairness, and trust.

8.

What Style of Parent Are You?

"Give me a break!" (Andrew, 18).

HOW MUCH AUTHORITY do you have, and use, as a parent?

How you answer this question can tell you a lot about your attitude toward, and relationship with, your teenager. When it comes to use of authority, parents usually use one of three parenting styles:

Authoritarian—"Do it my way or else . . . I'm the boss!"

Permissive—"Oh, do it your way . . . it's okay by me, I guess."

Authoritative—"I hear what you're saying, and I agree you're partially right. But I can't agree to everything you want. This time we'll do it this way because . . ." (explains reasoning).

These three approaches can be found in homes, Christian and otherwise, across the world. In fact, many parents see themselves using all three approaches, depending on the situation, their blood pressure, or the time of day.

For most people—teenagers and parents—the authoritative style sounds the best. It offers balance, and we all like to be balanced. I know I do. Trouble is, living with a teenager is quite often anything but a "balanced" proposition. Let's take a quick look at the three styles to see why an authoritative balance is not always so easy to maintain and why it's quite common to wander between permissive and authoritarian in the well-known no-man's-land called inconsistency.

129

"As Long As You're Under My Roof . . ."

Almost 30 percent of the teenagers I talked with described their parents with authoritarian terms.

"Obey me . . . don't talk back to me!" (Debbie, 13).

"When my sister and I fight, they threaten to send us to boarding school" (Carrie, 15).

"My dad uses 'As long as you live under my roof . . .' and it makes me feel like I'm not wanted" (Jennie, 16).

"That's it exactly—'You'll obey the rules, I'm the boss'—that or run away are my choices" (Brad, 15).

Christian and secular psychologists describe authoritarian parents as the kind who are usually long on use of the rod and short on use of dialog. For the authoritarian, to obey is a virtue, and punishment is swift for self-willfulness or crossing those in charge. Authoritarian parents insist that the child should take their word for what is right. Verbal give and take is definitely not encouraged.[1]

The authoritarian parent is strong on control, but weak on support, or love.[2] The child reared in a truly authoritarian home is usually clear on the name of the game: any back talk or stepping out of line and he gets it on the back side or "aside the head."

"Okay [Sigh], Have It Your Way"

Permissive parents are at the other end of the spectrum from authoritarian. Psychologists describe permissive parents as making few demands for orderly behavior and fulfilling responsibilities. Permissive parents do not punish, and are very agreeable with just about anything the child wants to do. They see themselves as a resource the child can use, rather than shapers of his behavior. Permissive parents allow the child to run his own show and do not make an issue of rules or standards. If push comes to shove, permissive parents allow the child to push and shove. They do not use power to control him, instead they appeal to reason.[3]

It is no surprise that the permissive parent is strong on support (love) but weak on control.[4] For the permissive child the name of the game is "have my own way," and he does.

About 10 percent of the teenagers in my survey pegged one parent or the other as permissive. Their comments indicate that at the teenage level the permissive parent sometimes plays psychological games with the child, with mixed results:

"They usually let me do what I want, but keep telling me over and over how they feel about things, which forces me to want to do things my way more" (Valerie, 17).

"They understand and let me do it my way, but sometimes they play to make you feel guilty, and you go their way" (Heidi, 15).

"Sometimes my mother cops out and says, 'Fire me,' or 'Do it your way'" (Steven, 15).

"Mom uses sarcasm, like if I ask to do something and she doesn't want me to, she'll say, 'Oh, go ahead—do what *you* want!'" (Ron, 15).

Sometimes the permissive approach can leave the teenager feeling neglected: Pam, 16, said: "Both my parents are permissive, they show no interest in my life. Whatever I want to do is okay with them. In a way they give me too much freedom."

Bad Results from Both Extremes

It is easy to predict the problems that can be caused by authoritarian and permissive parenting. The child reared in the authoritarian home may rebel, run away, or exist in an atmosphere of constant fear and hate. If he does survive the rigors of his own childhood he often goes on to become a harsh disciplinarian himself and the cycle repeats itself. Or, because he despised his own upbringing, he will shift all the way over to permissive parenting, which can often produce the classic spoiled brat.

Ironically, psychological researchers have discovered that both approaches can produce a child with still another basic problem: inability to interact with people. The child reared in the authoritarian atmosphere has learned he can never meet all the demands placed upon him; he is not to talk back or to question; he is to do things for himself with no help from others; he is to meet high standards at all times. The child from the permissive home has learned that life makes few demands; his wishes are always granted; he can always get plenty of help and doesn't need to be self-reliant. Standards are low and easy to meet.

Both kinds of children are not well equipped to deal with the real world, because both styles of parenting have minimized dissent. Authoritarian parents kill dissent by crushing it; permissive parents never give the child an opportunity to dissent because they are always diverting or indulging him.[5]

The Inconsistency Trap

While it's easy to spot the weaknesses in authoritarian and permissive styles of parenting, it is not easy to avoid them. Many parents wind up on a kind of sliding scale of inconsistency— permissive to a point, then getting fed up and cracking down with authoritarian wrath. In one group of fifty parents I worked with, half the class admitted to some degree of inconsistency. I confessed to them that I struggle with inconsistency too. Basically I want to be a good guy; I want my children to love me; I want to be, as they put it, "cool." All too often I slip into a permissive attitude and before I can say "authoritarian" the situation has escalated to where stronger measures are needed to preserve the peace, my marriage, or my sanity.

For example, my daughter Kim still talks about "the battle of the yardwork" that erupted one summer day when she was in junior high. I had drifted along in a permissive stupor for several weeks, as the weeds grew thicker and higher.

"When are you going to get the yard cleaned up?" Jackie asked me one Saturday. "It's a jungle out there."

I had to agree she was right. "The kids haven't been doing their weeding," I observed brilliantly. "Why does the yard always have to be such a hassle?"

Warming to the subject (and my little wife's prodding) I started through the house trying to sign up my three healthy, able-bodied children in the war against the weeds. But my impassioned enlistment speeches met with deaf ears, downturned mouths and eyeballs rolled to the ceiling (Jeff was the best eyeball-roller of all time). Finally, I had had it.

"All right, everybody—out there right *now*. We are going to weed that yard until it's done, and that's *IT!*"

Kim, Jeff, and Todd could tell by the *"IT"* that their time had come. The decibels had reached the danger tone. They reported reluctantly to the yard and received their weapons: one old screwdriver for slaying the enemy in hand-to-weed combat and one cardboard box for collecting the uprooted bodies.

The day wore on and the sun rose higher. Troop morale flagged. Kim started to sob softly as she stabbed dejectedly at a stubborn dandelion that refused to surrender.

"I don't see why I have to do this," she wailed. "The boys never help in the house!"

"Well, they will from now on," I promised grimly. "Keep going. Nobody stops until we're done."

The boys groaned; Kim sniffled. I felt guilty, but we weeded on until not a weed remained standing. As someone once said: "War is hell."

A goodly number of the teenagers I surveyed would recognize the above scene. Their parents often use a mixture of permissive and authoritarian approaches. Sometimes one parent would be authoritarian, the other permissive.

Doug, a college freshman, labeled his parents, "authoritarian and permissive, it depends on the situation."

Donna, a high school senior said her father was authoritarian—"especially if he's mad at me"—and her mother was permissive.

Carolyn, a high school sophomore, described her dad as "pretends to use authoritarian, but in the end is soft."

Stacey, a high school freshman, described her father as authoritarian, her mother, permissive. She comments: "My mom and dad are almost opposites, so sometimes when Mom says yes, Dad might say no and then it stays no—and *sometimes* vice versa.''

And so it goes in a lot of families. Parents ride some kind of authoritarian-permissive seesaw, as they cope with endless needs, requests, crises, and problems that are best labeled, ''never quite heard of *this* one before.''

It is clear that Paul did not have authoritarian or permissive parenting styles in mind when he penned Ephesians 6:4. What Paul was after was balance: high support and love (not exasperating or discouraging the child) *and* high control (bringing him up in the training and discipline of the Lord).

The Authoritative Happy Medium

Psychological research reveals the authoritative parent as someone who is the boss but willing to listen. To parent authoritatively is to be open to questions and to explain your reasoning and policies. Authoritative parents are in control but not oppressively restrictive. They recognize their own rights and those of the child. They are a comfortable blend of ''reasonable'' but ''firm when it's necessary.''[6]

The authoritative parent takes the strengths of the authoritarian and permissive parent and combines them to be high on support (love) and high on control.[7] Like a lot of other ''sound psychology'' authoritative parenting is just good common sense, especially when you have teenagers. The teenager is at a point where he is questioning everything and everyone. He is not too interested in obedience for obedience' sake. Now he wants to know ''Why should I?'' Verbal give and take is the name of his game, and if you don't let him play, you have the makings of rebellion or, at least, sullen resignation.

All this new-found independence usually occurs in junior high, sometimes a little before. It seems to arrive with puberty, zits, and sudden fierce loyalty to the peer group. A survey of 150 junior-high students reported 36 percent as "very dependent" on their families, while 58 percent said "sometimes dependent." When the same group was asked if they respected their parents' ideas and opinions, 76 percent answered "sometimes" while only 20 percent checked "all the time."[8]

The above statistics don't necessarily make a case for all junior high students, but these answers do indicate that younger teenagers are starting to flex their wings and strut around the nest a bit. They can be critical and often tactless as they challenge authority at home. Many parents aren't ready for this at all.

"What's going on with the kid?" a father asks in bewilderment. "All of a sudden I have to start giving him *reasons* for things?"

Some parents read their youngster's demands for reasons and explanations as smart talk or that old favorite, "teenage rebellion." They crack down with a get-tough policy, but it doesn't seem to do all that much good.

We found this especially true when Jeff was in junior high. The neat, reasonable answers I had been putting in my books for teenagers didn't seem to compute for Jeff. The cool, laid-back detachment that I had when talking to other people's teenagers melted under the heat of some kind of electrical force field that sprung up between us. Had I better understood what was going on, I could have handled his "orneriness" a lot better. I know from experience that using power to establish your authority with a teenager has limited results.

One simple question I might have used more with Jeff in junior high is, "Why not?" Then I could have used active listening and reflecting of feelings to see what was bugging him. That way I could have learned what didn't seem fair or reasonable to him and he could have understood my needs better, too. As he got into senior high I started using this approach more often, learning slowly by trial and error. Sometimes it worked, other times I struck out and wound up in a confrontation that undermined my authority rather than building it.

"My Parents Are Authoritative—Sort of"

Over 50 percent of the young people I surveyed reported that their parents used the authoritative approach to parenting, to some degree.

Larry, 14 and in the ninth grade, lives with his mother. His dad died when he was five. He says: "She usually tries to see it my way, but if she can't, she likes me to do it her way."

Eugene, 16, reports: "My dad will sometimes use this (the authoritative) style. He'll sometimes say, 'Well, we'll do it somewhat your way, but I still want to try my way.'"

Dawn, 18, saw her parents as authoritative ". . . but often they are willing to listen to my opinion and let me do it my way, knowing that the experience of making my own choice is good for me sometimes."

Ron, 19, had parents who apparently combined some form of active listening with authoritative style: "My parents would listen to what I had to say, and then decide they would *really* listen."

With many of the teenagers I surveyed, it was clear that their parents weren't 100 percent authoritative. Like most human beings they struggled to stay on the firm ground of happy medium, but sometimes slipped toward too tough or too easy.

Ken, 15, went down the list of choices on his questionnaire and checked authoritative for his parents, but then added: "Pretty much a mixture."

Craig's parents were divorced when he was 14, and he has not seen his father since. Now, at 19, he sees his mother as having been, "usually authoritative, but when irate she'll say she doesn't care (very effective)."

Jeff, 13, believes his parents were authoritative, "most of the time and I understand why." He did say that sometimes they were authoritarian and, "You've got to learn to live with it."

Debi's parents divorced when she was five. Now, at 15, she lives with her mother and says, "I think she is authoritative toward me, and I like that." At the same time she calls her mother "inconsistent" with discipline. "Some days she'll let me get away with not doing the dishes and the next day she'll get mad because I don't do them.''

A message coming through in the above comments is that parents try to be authoritative (firm but fair), but in the eyes of their teenagers they still grapple with inconsistency. I didn't get to ask their parents how *they* saw it, but chances are they would agree— to a point. It is hard to always call the shots just right. Unless you are a total authoritarian, with no concern but that your word be law, there are always the gnawing questions: "Was I too tough? Too permissive? Was I really fair? Am I doing this according to Scripture?"

Ridenour Rides Again—at 2:30 A.M.

I have already described our curfew problems with Jeff throughout high school. Compared to other parents we were quite lenient, but still could seldom get Jeff home "on time." He would come in anywhere from 15 to 45 minutes late, sometimes even later. "Don't do the crime if you can't do the time," I would intone and logical consequences would follow—grounding or no use of the car. But nothing seemed to work.

As Todd moved into high school he did not have as big a problem with curfew as Jeff did; he usually was home on time or before. But on some occasions, particularly over weekends, he would bristle and mutter about "not always knowing what time it might be over." By this he meant it was hard to put a limit on whatever might be happening with his friends. We never worried about drugs or drinking, but we knew he didn't like having to say "Sorry, gotta get home *right now.*"

I have worked on this book through much of Todd's senior year in high school. As basketball season went into its final weeks, Todd's team played the cross-town rivals in a crucial game. (Games with cross-town rivals are always crucial, but this one was especially so.) A starting forward, Todd had a game high 18 rebounds and made two clutch baskets in the final minutes to put the game away.

It was a Friday night and Jackie and I went home to bed. Todd would be in before midnight, we were sure, because a schedule rearrangement made it necessary for Todd's team to play their other cross-town rival the very next night.

We went to sleep and at 1:00 A.M. the phone rang. I answered it but got no reply, only a click. A girl wanting Todd's autograph? A burglar wanting to see if we weren't home? No matter, Todd wasn't in yet so I lay there awake, assuming he would be along in a minute, and, according to our custom, knock on the door and tell me he was in.

A half hour went by and the phone rang again. Again, nobody was there. Todd wasn't either. By this time I was getting a bit uneasy. His old Toyota had faithfully labored beyond 100,000 miles. Was this the night it had decided to have a coronary? Or was it a flat tire? Maybe he was out of gas. Like a lot of teenagers he lived hand to gas tank, often counting on getting home on fumes.

As the minutes ticked on, so did my fertile imagination: a wreck? car trouble? Perhaps some of the cruder fellows from the losing school had mugged him for his part in the victory. Finally, at 1:58 I called his buddy, Ric. Yes, he and Todd had gone to their favorite pizza parlor after the game to celebrate. Yes, Todd had left a little early. With whom? Ric didn't know.

The plot thickened and so did my concern as I lay there in dialogue with myself:

"Don't be such a mother hen, he's big enough to take care of himself."

"*You're right, but what about those weird phone calls?*"

"Kids are always playing games on the phone. Look, if he's old enough to be drafted, he's old enough to be out late."

"*I suppose, but he's never been this late and he hasn't called. Maybe he's stranded and can't get to a phone. . . .*"

At 2:13 I could wait no longer. I got dressed and shuffled out to the car to "go out and look for my son." (We could call the cops a bit later.) I drove to the shopping center just half a mile away and went past the pizza parlor where Todd had been just an hour or two before. It was dark now, with all the pizza dough tucked in for the night. Oh that Todd were home tucked in as well (not to mention his father). Strangely, I wasn't really angry, just rather weary and getting more and more worried.

Before starting down several main roads where Todd might be stranded, I thought it worthwhile to stop at an all-night restaurant near the shopping center and phone headquarters for an update. At 2:28 I dialed our number and heard Jackie's welcome words: "He's home, came in a few minutes ago. He and Suzanne were talking." (Suzanne? Todd had no girlfriend and seldom had dated through his senior year. He did know a Suzanne who was more in the category of a friend . . .) "The time got away from him," Jackie explained. "He said he was sorry."

And so Colombo Ridenour's case was solved. I drove home and parked the car. I trudged up the steps and past Todd's door. He had talked with his mother; tomorrow would be soon enough to talk with me. I did talk with God. The main topic was gratitude.

The next afternoon we did talk. As we sat down I wondered about how to handle this one. An "I" message perhaps, like "I'm getting a little too old to run search and rescue missions at 2:30 in the morning." How would I walk that authoritative line, never wandering into the slough of authoritarian or permissive despond?

"I want to talk about last night," I began. "I was pretty worried when you didn't get in by at least 1:00 o'clock. We had two odd phone calls, too."

Todd looked blank as I described the phone calls. "I guess I blew it" was his main comment.

"Yeah, you did kind of blow it," I agreed. "Your mom and I worry . . . I know you think you're indestructible, but the car is old. I could see you with a flat, or out of gas or broken down somewhere. I wish you would have phoned us or something . . ."

"Yeah, I guess I should have, but I didn't realize it was that late. We just got to talking. . . ."

"You still don't have a watch? I thought I gave you one of my old ones a while back."

"I think I lost it . . . yeah, I guess I could use a watch."

"And a dime," I added. "Really, we don't make that big a deal out of curfew, but 2:30 is too late and even if the next day is Saturday and you got to sleep in, you've got another game to play tonight. Frankly, you should have been home a lot earlier. In the future let's work on calling if you're going to be late. Is that fair?''

"Yeah, I guess so."

That was about it. Now, I'm not sure how I came out. I realize some parents might chuckle a bit hysterically at this story. Oh, if only all they had to worry about was a rare instance of coming in an hour or so later than "the limit." Other parents might suggest a firmer hand: no car privileges for a week or two, some kind of grounding, etc.

But I don't think so. You recall I mentioned playing the grounding game with Jeff for years with little results. Besides, Todd's track record had been quite good, and at this point—senior in high school recently turned 18—taking away the car would be, as the teenagers put it, "pretty cold." If this had happened at age 13 or 14 or even 16, some logical consequences might have been in order. But in this case I got my point across. He had blown it; he knew he had gone past the limits. And although I had not flexed my parental authority, he knew I wouldn't be too happy with a repeat performance of the graveyard patrol.

As I see it, I was authoritative, perhaps drifting toward permissive. Some may see me as too soft, not definite enough. Could be, but I would rather err on the side of letting my 18-year-old preserve his dignity and self-esteem rather than protect his father's ego. If I am serious about the deparenting plan mentioned in earlier chapters, I am willing to risk giving my son opportunities to handle limits and the luxury of making some mistakes.

I do have to admit I'm not sure how I came out on the "give-and-take" side of it. According to the theory, the "ideal authoritative parent" allows his child opportunities for give-and-take, and they both meet their needs. But the theories and ideals have a way of muddling up for me. As I think about it, I guess there was "give-and-take": I *took* a certain amount of worry and inconvenience and I *gave* quite a bit of forgiveness. But I survived, and since the night of the 2:30 caper Todd has been out late hardly at all. And, he's even phoned a couple of times to tell us where he is and what time he'll be home. (That reminds me, I've got to check to see if he ever found his watch.)

Wobbly Legs Are Better Than None

When it comes to walking the authoritative tightrope, I like what Jim Dobson says in *The Strong-Willed Child.* In a refreshingly candid chapter entitled "The Strong-Willed Adolescent (Is There Any Other Kind?)" Dobson admits parents don't really have much power over teenagers. He writes:

"After we have appealed to reason and cooperation and family loyalty, all that remains are relatively weak methods of 'punishment.' We can only link behavior of our kids with desirable and undesirable consequences and hope the connection will be of sufficient influence to elicit their cooperation.

"If that sounds pretty wobbly-legged, let me admit what I am implying: a willful, angry, sixteen-year-old boy or girl CAN win a confrontation with his parents today. The law leans ever more in the direction of emancipation of the teenager."[9]

Jim Dobson sounding a bit wobbly-legged? Not really. As he points out, in certain states teenagers can leave home and not be forced to return, and they can obtain birth control pills or abortions without parental knowledge or consent, to name just some of the "adult" privileges available to them. The odds are on the teenager's side and getting better all the time.

Authoritative parents do not wield power like a club; they use reason and logic, and trust the Lord for the plays that are too close to call. The authoritative parent may sometimes seem to be on wobbly legs, but better to look a little wobbly-legged than be without a leg to stand on.

Key Attitude #8: Self-Control

When Paul wrote Ephesians 6:4 he was capsulizing the balance taught throughout the Bible. Scripture has many examples of the folly in using power selfishly and unwisely. David tried it with Bathsheba, then murdered Uriah to cover up his lust (2 Sam. 11). But David's sins were discovered and later he paid with the death of his son (2 Sam. 12).

Solomon's son, Rehoboam, tried it when he listened to the young men who gave him foolish counsel to make the burden of the Israelites even heavier than his father had. Rehoboam "scourged the people with scorpions" and in no time at all he split the Kingdom asunder (1 Kings 12). In one foolish misuse of authority he caused rebellion, rivalry, weakness, and misery that lasted for centuries.

David and Rehoboam are glaring examples of lack of self-control. The person with self-control uses authority to serve, build, and nurture, not to pillage and take power trips. Jesus taught His disciples with "authority, and not as the scribes" (Matt. 7:29, KJV), but He never taught the virtues of misusing power. He knew that people in authority have power, but He taught that the truly blessed are the meek and the peacemakers (Matt. 5:5, 9).

Unfortunately, too many parents don't relate very well to being meek. Our twentieth-century concept of meekness pictures a namby-pamby permissiveness that seeks peace at any price. The biblical meaning of meek, however, is "mild of temper, patient under injury, gentle, and kind." The authoritative parent can be meek but still be in control because he has self-control. Actually, he is under Christ-control. Through His Holy Spirit, Christ provides the strength to cope with the frustrations of parenting. I can't be sure, but perhaps the Lord included self-control as part of the fruit of the Spirit just for parents. He knew we would need it.

All of this makes a tidy Bible lesson and a very big point about how to parent teenagers. The authoritative parent uses *self-control,* not to manipulate or dominate, but to nurture and train. It takes self-control to make your plan for deparenting work. As the plan for deparenting chart shows (see page 143), your teenager already has a certain amount of freedom and responsibility, but you can be sure that he or she is reaching for more. The way the teenager reaches for more freedom is to start bargaining more aggressively in that area called "negotiable responsibility." For example, he may want his own car, but can't quite afford it; she may want to go steady, but you are not so sure. It is this kind of negotiating that puts any parent's self-control to the test. To parent authoritatively you are to nurture as you negotiate, but not drive your teenager to discouragement, or worse.

And right about here you may be wondering: "To be authoritative and have self-control sounds great. I certainly don't want to manipulate and dominate my teenagers, but then I don't want to be manipulated and dominated by them either. Teenagers are not adults; they need guidance. They sometimes make unreasonable demands and don't always use sound judgment. What happens when they really blow it? What about discipline? What happens when push comes to shove and I have to call the close ones as I see them?"

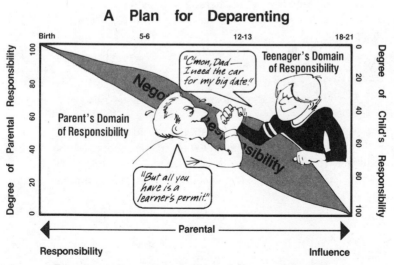

Teenagers can be aggressive bargainers in the area of negotiable responsibility.

Those are all good questions and the strategy for answering them authoritatively is in chapter 9.

FOR THOUGHT, DISCUSSION, AND ACTION

1. Analyze when you are authoritarian, when you are permissive, and when you try to be authoritative. Is there a certain pattern that leads you into an unbalanced position—too authoritarian or too permissive?

2. How comfortable is it for you to think about having less and less power over your teenager? How do you really feel about your teenager's growing independence?

3. Following is a brief quiz to help you identify your parenting style. Check the statements that sound closest to what you might say to your teenager:

1. "As long as you live here, you obey the rules."
2. "You came in 30 minutes after curfew last night. What happened?"
3. "Well, this *is* a great game. I guess you can stay up to watch even if it is a school night."
4. "Don't do the crime if you can't do the time."
5. "Oh, go ahead and use the car. I'll get a ride with someone else."
6. "Don't ask so many questions . . . just do it!"
7. "You're right, I jumped to conclusions about your buddy, but how are we going to work out your schedule with his?"
8. "Enough of that! If you can't speak with a civil tongue, don't speak at all!"
9. "Sounds like you are pretty upset with me. Give me the whole story."
10. "You're late because you overslept and you want me to give you a special ride to school? Well, okay, I guess."
11. "Okay, we'll try it your way this time. I'm willing to see how you can handle it."

12. "Okay, have it your way. Call me if you need any help."
13. "Let's both cool off and talk about this again later."
14. "I understand that it's a big deal and everyone is going, but I need a little more information."
15. "Okay, okay, there's no need to talk that way to your mother."

For answers that identify each statement as authoritarian, permissive, or authoritative, see Appendix 4, page 201.

9.

When Somebody Has to Call the Shots

"I love them very much for the times they have corrected me"
(Gail, 17).

QUESTION: What's the best way to discipline a teenager?

To hear the teenagers tell it, the answer is: very carefully—and always fairly. It's not hard to find teenagers who are less than pleased with how their parents use discipline, control, and authority.

A college student said: "I need to leave them because they have been *too* restrictive on me to the point where my counselor feels that I will "flake out" if I don't get on my own to try out my wings. I love them a lot, but it's time that I leave" (Marcia, 18).

Mike, a freshman at a Christian university wrote: "Give me a chance to speak and give my point of view, even if it is irrelevant."

Craig, a sophomore at the same school, had a similar plea: "Be patient and look at my point of view so we can discuss and comprehend our problems and it will be worked out."

I asked one group of junior- and senior-high students if they ever won in conflicts with their parents. Did their parents ever compromise at some points?

Debbie, 13, has authoritarian parents who want her to do things their way because "they think their way is right." Her answer: "No."

Brad, 15, also has authoritarian parents who use "very little" of his opinion. His answer: "No . . . no."

146

Suzie, 14, said: "Most of the time they win, since I don't really care as long as I don't have to listen anymore. But it doesn't seem like anyone really 'wins.'"

Jennie, 16, answered: "I can't recall ever winning any conflicts."

Becky, 15, admitted: "Those conversations usually end up in tears."

Other teenagers, however, had various reasons for feeling better about conflicts and compromising:

Pam, 16, has permissive parents and when there are conflicts, she says: "I usually win because they always give in. They don't fight back."

Rhonda, 14, says her parents compromise with her to some extent. "I say I'll do something for them if I can do what I want."

Chris, 14: "Yes, most of the time I win. Sometimes we compromise. For example, I want to stay out with friends until 12:00. My parents want me home at 10:00. I stay out till 11:00."

Scott, 14: "Sometimes I win, but sometimes I don't understand something that I did wrong, so they need to explain it to me."

Daniel, 13: "Sometimes—when I want to go somewhere—my parents are busy. If I can work things out, I can go."

Judy, 15: "Oh sure. I don't remember what they were about, but I have heard them say, 'She's right.'"

One of the most positive remarks came from Pam, a 16-year-old high-school junior, who said: "We have a great relationship and are able to work out our differences."

Teenagers Face a Catch-22

To be able to "work out our differences" is a key goal for the parent who wants to use authority with a teenager in a wise and fair fashion. As I talked with teenagers across the country a basic pitfall came to light: many parents discipline their teenagers in the same way they disciplined them when they were preadolescents. This is particularly true of parents with teenagers in junior high. Junior high is often a baffling time for the teenager and the parent.

The sweet little girl or obedient little boy from elementary years is replaced by a budding teenager whose body is undergoing, or already has undergone, radical changes due to puberty. Adolescence has sprouted, along with the drive for independence. Authoritative parenting—being willing to engage in give-and-take and give reasons "why"—is the best way to go, but it is not easy. Plans for deparenting and negotiating responsibility, discussed in earlier chapters, often seem futile, or so difficult and time consuming they aren't worth the trouble.

And so, at the most critical time of his life, the 13- to 15-year-old moves through a sequence of developments that follow along these lines:

1. The teenager "changes." He may become silent, moody, and withdrawn. He usually starts questioning and challenging authority in one way or another.

2. The teenager starts going to his peer group for his values and guidelines. He is not necessarily tossing out everything his parents taught him; he is testing, experimenting, trying to figure out who he really is.

3. The parent feels his authority is being threatened when his teenager acts "out of control," even in a mild form.

4. The parent decides he'd better crack down before this "wild animal" gets completely out of hand.

5. The teenager does not appreciate the crack-down. He fights back, sometimes openly, and sometimes passively, but the war is on.

At the critical ages of 13, 14, and 15 the teenager finds himself in a Catch-22 situation. He needs love, support, and understanding, but because he's acting in unlovable ways, everyone—especially parents and teachers—seems to crack down on him. The above sequence does not happen to every junior-high teenager, but it happens to many. It is no wonder that Dr. James Dobson, who once taught junior high grades, says, "What a shame that *most* teenagers decide that they are without much human worth when they're between 13 and 15 years of age!"[1]

For many young people, things don't get a whole lot better as they hit high school and college. Kim, a 16-year-old junior in high school, complains: "My parents gave me too much freedom when I was younger. Now that I have started dating and going out, finally getting into the real world, they're trying to put controls on me."

Eric, an 18-year-old college freshman, felt tension the last two years of high school, for a different reason. "My parents became interested in what I was doing, but we hadn't been communicating for so long there wasn't much of a base for understanding why I was doing things in my life and what they wanted me to do."

Greg, 19, also a college freshman remembers, "I can see a lot of situations where I thought I had all the answers and my parents were wrong. I can see now there were a lot of times when my dad didn't fully explain himself and that's why I didn't always understand what he was saying. Also, there were times when my dad didn't want to admit he was wrong. First he would say, 'No' and then I would say, 'What about this or this?' But I could tell that he just didn't want to back down even though he knew that what I had come up with would be okay and that maybe his first judgment wasn't quite right. I could sense he just didn't want to give in to that."

The telltale symptoms are plain: trying to suddenly put on controls, no base for understanding, not wanting to give in. Parents struggle with use of authority and letting go. The conflicts come thick and fast and cause friction and tension. Often the parent uses the only technique he knows—he tightens the screw of authority to keep the teenager under control. But it's a losing battle.

There are better methods for working with teenagers, who are, after all, a lot like parents. They like being treated fairly and considerately. We've already looked at one excellent method in chapter 6—active listening. Two other good methods are the "I" message and a system for resolving conflicts. First, a look at the "I" message.

"I" Messages Confront Instead of Attack

The "I" message is a tool taught by various communicators and parenting specialists.[2] Using the "I" message works like this:

    1. The parent needs to confront the teenager with a complaint

or problem of some kind. The teenager has done, or not done, something that makes the parent unhappy, concerned, etc. Often, this same problem has happened before and has reached the stage where something has to be done. For example, the bathroom is a disaster area again and the last one to use it was the teenager.

2. The primary value of the ''I'' message is that it replaces the typical ''you'' message, which puts the teenager on the defensive. For example, Mom finds the mess in the bathroom, but instead of saying, ''You are too much. This mess is unbelievable. Will you always be a slob?'' She sends an ''I'' message instead:

''I'm irritated by this mess in the bathroom, because I get tired of cleaning up after everyone.''

The relationship between ''you'' messages and many of the Communication Killers discussed in chapter 5 is clear. Gunslinger Words, Defensive Words, Nagging Words, etc. often come in the form of ''you'' messages. The usual result is that the teenager feels attacked, put down, or ''bad'' to some degree. His natural response is to send a ''you'' message of his own, such as, ''You aren't always that neat yourself'' or ''Why do you always have to be so fussy?''

What you hope to accomplish with an ''I'' message, however, is to confront, not attack. Instead of passing all kinds of judgments, the parent shares his feelings about the situation. And, of course, the teenager is invited to send back an ''I'' message of his own to communicate how he might feel. Using ''I'' messages takes courage. The parent has to be open about feelings and at times share weaknesses like, ''I'm tired'' or ''I'm angry'' or ''I just can't handle this . . .'' And, it takes courage to allow the teenager his right to an ''I'' message, which may be quite blunt or even hurtful.

Below are more situations and typical ''you'' messages that a parent might send. Read them over, then think of an ''I'' message you can send instead:

1. Fourteen-year-old leaves gate to street open again and two-year-old brother gets clear out to the curb before teenager spots him. He grabs little brother just in time, as Mom looks on in horror.

"You" message: "You are irresponsible! What are you trying to do, kill your baby brother?"

"I" message (write in your own):

2. Parent is repulsed by outfit son or daughter plans to wear to school.

"You" message: "Are you going to school in *that?* Don't you have any respect for the teachers, or for us?"

"I" message (write in your own):

3. Sixteen-year-old uses Dad's tools to fix his motorcycle but forgets to put them away.

"You" message: "Come out here and explain why you are always losing my tools. Can't you learn to be considerate?"

"I" message (write in your own):

As you look back over your version of an "I" message in each situation keep in mind what an "I" message is not.

An "I" message does not always convey only a negative feeling. For example, instead of telling the careless babysitter, "I'm really upset. Jimmy could have been killed," a better approach would be: "I was scared to death, but I'm proud of you for acting so fast. Little Jimmy could have been run over. I'm worried it will happen again. Can I count on you to help?"

An "I" message is not a cover-up for venting anger. For example, "I'm really fed up with that kind of outfit. I want it changed—now!" is shooting from the hip. Better to say: "I'm uncomfortable with what you're wearing. I'd like to know your reasoning and if there isn't something else we could both be happy with."

An "I" message should not be a first-person version of attacking or blaming the teenager. For example, "I'm really upset with

my tools always missing. I think you are irresponsible'' is a
''you'' message in disguise and not much of a disguise at that. A
better approach would be: ''I'm disappointed that the tools are
missing again, because I get tired of always having to look for
them.''

Like active listening, sending ''I'' instead of ''you'' messages
is not something you master in one or two simple lessons. A lot
depends on your tone of voice and the look on your face. The
primary rule is to express your feelings, but without put-downs
and cutting judgments, without calling names and laying blame.

Keep in mind also that you should use ''I'' messages sparingly,
when your goal is to resolve a problem or conflict that is truly
irritating. Don't send an ''I'' message to your teenager unless you
have the determination or energy to work through the problem.
Granted, sometimes schedules may not allow you to deal with the
problem on the spot. For example, you find the mess in the bathroom and send the ''I'' message. But you are due at work and your
teenager is due at school. Your teenager promises ''to clean it up
later,'' and you say, ''That's a temporary solution, but tonight
after dinner I want to talk about how we can keep the bathroom
neater instead of letting it get like this.''

You may have to work with ''I'' messages for a while before
they seem to improve your communication with your teenager.
With some teenagers it may not make much difference. The
younger the child when you start to use ''I'' messages the better.
But regardless of how effective an ''I'' message may or may not
be, it is a vastly superior approach to ''you'' messages, which are
almost guaranteed to cut off communication before it can start.

Working Out the Differences

When used with care, ''I'' messages are a valuable way to
confront problems and get them out on the table, but that's only a
start. There is still the question of how you solve the situation. You
can confront a teenager about a messy bathroom by using an ''I''
message, but there is no guarantee that he or she will suddenly

repent of slob-like ways and become an impeccable joy. What you need is a system for discussing problems and working out differences together.

Gary J. Hess, who developed the Plan for Deparenting introduced in chapter 3, teaches the following conflict-resolution process in courses and seminars he conducts to help professional teachers gain better communication skills. Gary has used the same system with his own teenagers, who are now both in college. Here's an outline of how it works:

1. Clarify the problem. (Find out what's wrong.)
2. Clarify needs. (Send "I" message, then actively listen.)
3. Generate possible solutions. (The parent and teenager *both* contribute.)
4. Mutually agree on a solution. (Use the authoritative give-and-take style.)
5. Implement the solution. (Try it for a day, a week, etc.)
6. Evaluate the results. (Do this as soon as possible.)
   a. If solution is working, give positive reinforcement.
   b. If solution is not working, build in logical consequences.

Gary's system is similar to one taught by Thomas Gordon in his book, *Parent Effectiveness Training,* except for one important difference. Dr. Gordon is completely against use of authority by the parent. He equates "authority" with "power" and uses the words interchangeably. In chapter 10 of his book Gordon makes a strong statement against use of authority by parents, claiming that the parent must give up all power in order to achieve a "no-lose" situation. He believes that if parent and child work on a conflict long enough they will eventually resolve it to everyone's satisfaction.[3]

In the authoritative approach taught by Gary, the parent and teenager work out a mutually satisfactory solution and then try it out. If the teenager does his part the parent expresses appreciation (gives positive reinforcement). If the solution is not working and the problem continues, the parent introduces logical consequences as a form of training and discipline, not punishment.

The Great Phone Debate

For example, when Gary's daughter, Mindy, was in junior high and her sister, Brenda, was in sixth grade, use of the telephone became a major problem. The girls were tying up the phone for an hour to two hours per night, talking to friends. Gary and Lola needed to have the phone clear during part of each evening to receive important calls concerning church activities, Gary's work, etc.

After identifying the issue, Gary sent the girls an "I" message: "I am frustrated with the amount of time you are spending on the phone, because Mom and I need to have the line clear to get important calls."

So Gary and the girls sat down to think of solutions. Mindy and Brenda thought it would be great if each could have a private line. That way everybody would have a phone.

Gary thought it would be great if the girls could agree to stay off the phone between the hours of 7 and 9 P.M. each night.

The girls countered by saying that was prime time for calls, and they just couldn't cut all calls during those hours.

Gary asked the girls how they would pay for their own private phones (at the time they were getting something like two dollars a week in allowance).

Finally everyone agreed to a solution: Mindy and Brenda would take or make phone calls in the evening, but never spend more than ten minutes on any one call. Then they would have to wait at least ten minutes before accepting or making another call. This would leave the phone open for a certain amount of time to allow calls for Mom and Dad to come through.

They tried the plan and it worked—sort of. There were nights when the girls did not watch the clock too carefully. Gary re-evaluated the problem with them and they agreed together that abuse of the ten-minute rule would result in a logical consequence:

no more phone calls that particular night. The plan worked fairly well after that. Gary remembers only one or two evenings when the "no calls this evening" consequence was invoked. Gary does admit that he and Lola did more clock minding than the girls did, but he believes it was worth it to give his daughters experience in conflict resolution and gaining more responsibility.

Now, you may be thinking, "That seems like going to a lot of time and trouble. Why not just tell Mindy and Brenda "No phone calls after 8:00 P.M.," or maybe, "One phone call per night after dinner, period"? True that might be easier and more agreeable to the parent, but it would not be too appealing to the teenager. And, as most parents know, making a rule is not the end of it. Rules are for "getting around" or at least bending and few are more skilled in bending and skirting rules than teenagers. By involving the girls in the solution Gary guided them in developing responsibility instead of simply ordering them to be responsible.

By invoking logical consequences, Gary maintained his position as nurturing parent, authoritative but reasonable. "But aren't logical consequences little more than a threat or a punishment?" you may ask. Of course, logical consequences can be used that way. It's up to the parent. The positive use of logical consequences is to teach exactly what the name describes. Life is full of consequences for certain acts, and they logically happen when certain things are done or not done.

Every System Has Weak Spots

Like any "system" the conflict resolution plan described above has its problems and its leaks. No skill or system is airtight, for one good reason: it is being used by human beings. And in this case they are trying to accomplish a task that is possibly the most difficult in life—communicating and getting along with each other. But just because a system has weaknesses does not mean it is not worth trying and practicing. Here are some of the more common pitfalls and questions about conflict resolution and how to deal with them:

1. *There is not enough time to resolve everything.* Life does not live that way. Not only is there not enough time to run every problem through the six steps; parent and teenager do not have the patience or energy to always do so. Gary Hess believes the typical parent has energy to resolve or negotiate no more than 15 to 20 percent of the teenager's behavior at any one time. How, then, do you handle the other 80 to 85 percent?

First, have an agreement with your teenager to be open to negotiating new areas or issues as they come up. Teenagers are often self-centered, but they are seldom stupid. If you show your teenager you are serious about your "give-and-take" policy, he or she will usually be willing to work with you instead of against you. (For more on this, see chapter 10.)

Parenting authoritatively takes an *equal* amount of control and love. When parents achieve a fairly good balance of control and love, they usually win the teenager's cooperation. Most of the teenagers I talked with were basically positive on being reared somewhere within the authoritative range:

Don, 14, said his parents use the authoritative style most of the time. "I don't usually get in conflicts with them," he wrote on his questionnaire, "but when I do, we usually come to an agreement." And he added: "The general way they treat me, I couldn't be more thankful for."

Nancy, 13, says her parents are authoritative most of the time. She wrote: "They explain what they want and sometimes let me choose the right one and sometimes command me to do what they say." Her general assessment: "I just love the way they brought me and my brothers and sisters up. They are great examples to me . . . I just praise the Lord for who they are."

Scott, who is 14, labels his parents as authoritative and says: "I think they want to show me that I'm right quite a bit of the time instead of always telling me I'm wrong. They really encourage me and (usually) always understand what is happening in my life. They really love me a lot!!!"

Carrie, 15, reported that her parents were strict but "pretty neat" about not controlling her too much. She says if she is ever a parent herself she will operate ". . . almost exactly like my parents." She hopes they will "Keep goin' like you're goin'."

Steven, who is also 15, said his parents were authoritative and willing to engage in give-and-take ". . . when I talk to them peaceably about a problem." He believes he sometimes wins in conflict situations when "I don't spout, but I think before I speak."

One thing the above comments show is that every family has to work out its own style of operating together. In the family that is parented authoritatively, give-and-take has to come from *both* sides. The teenager knows who is in charge, but he also knows he has an open forum and the right to question, challenge, and ask why. Life is never perfect. There are conflicts. You win some, you lose some, and sometimes you may arrive at an "ideal solution" where nobody feels he lost completely. If the balance of love and control is correct, those areas and issues that need negotiating and resolving usually stay within the 15 to 20 percent range.

You will notice I keep saying "usually." There are always exceptions. Some teenagers come at parents from every direction. There are days when you think *everything* is a conflict. I've had a few of those days myself. At times like that it might help to go over the suggestions for handling anger and frustration in chapter 7.

If necessary, "call time out," as my friend Gary Hess likes to put it. Sit down with your teenager and send some "I" messages. Invite his "I" messages in return. Actively listen for feelings and share your own. Phrases like "I love you" and "I care about you" go farther than all the plans and systems combined. Let your teenager know, "Our relationship is the most important thing—I want to make it work." You can work it out together—somehow.

2. *It is easy for the parent to bring a hidden agenda.* Resolving conflicts authoritatively takes discipline and self-control on the parent's part. After trying it for awhile, check on yourself. If you are winning every time because you "are always right" it is doubtful that your teenager sees this as very fair or much fun. If neither one of you can think of examples where you, the parent, are giving, even a little, you are not abiding by the ground rules,

which are designed to allow both of you to make points and gain concessions. You are simply using your authority and power in a thinly disguised form, and you are not achieving your main goal— the passing of responsibility from yourself to your teenager.

3. *Logical consequences should be logical and reasonable, not a club.* It is quite common to "resolve a conflict" but then find that the teenager has a hidden agenda of his own. He doesn't abide by the agreement. You may negotiate again, and send him an "I" message like, "I'm disappointed in your not doing the lawn (garbage, homework, etc. etc.) as we agreed. How can we work this out?" And so you try again, but there is still little improvement.

At this point the authoritative style calls for logical consequences, which should be used as a tool, not a weapon. Dr. Bruce Narramore defines logical consequences as ". . . some event or consequence that is agreed upon beforehand by the parent and teen which will come to pass if one's responsibilities are not fulfilled. For example, if your son is in charge of feeding the family pet and his job is not done by the time evening rolls around, it is logical that he does not have a meal either!"[4]

A logical consequence should always be directly related to the particular failure to meet a responsibility. For example: If you don't cut the grass, you don't go to the beach; if you don't wash the car, you don't use the car that week; if you stay out past curfew, you're grounded next time around. Dr. Narramore stresses that logical consequences should always be worked out *ahead of time with the teenager.* If possible, get the teenager to suggest the consequence himself. That way it will look more reasonable to him if and when it must be invoked.[5] This is part of understanding the ground rules. If everyone understands and agrees to the ground rules, there is less chance for bad feelings and charges of "unfair!"

When used correctly, logical consequences are valuable because they are similar to life's natural consequences.[6] If you jump out of a window, you break your leg, or worse. If you drive 85 miles per hour sooner or later you get a ticket, or even end up in jail. If you stay up late night after night, you become ill, cranky, or so punchy you can't function properly. The Scriptures teach logical consequences in Paul's pungent observation that we reap exactly what we sow (see Gal. 6:7). In many instances, logical consequences used in a family are a relatively less painful dress rehearsal for coping in the day-to-day world.

While a system of logical consequences helps teach the teenager what happens when responsibilities are not met, it is no panacea for all conflict problems. When I asked teenagers if their parents used logical consequences and how it worked, their answers usually suggested a mode of punishment, rather than training:

Pam, a seventh grader, reported one novel logical consequence used by her parents: if she failed in a responsibility, they would "choose her clothes for a week." Pam made no comment on how fair this was, but when asked how she would handle parenting if she ever had children, she said, "Differently . . . understand." And she added, "I'm a person, too, I have feelings."

Becky, 15, described use of logical consequences at her house like this: "My dad takes away some of our allowance. It doesn't work because he bugs us so much about doing our chores that we don't do them just to get back at him."

Daniel, 13, explained: "Sometimes they give me the choice for what my punishment is, but I don't like that."

Nancy, also 13, added: "They give the punishment as the rule is broken. I like this way 'cause lots of times if they use the 'logical consequence' they don't give you the time to explain yourself."

Use of logical consequences at our house obtained mixed results.

Kimberly, our oldest, was determined to not make mistakes; the thought of logical consequences was too horrible for her to contemplate. She recalls that when she was about 10 or 11 she went to a neighbor's house and stayed for an hour or two. We got concerned about her absence because she hadn't told us where she was going. When she got home, I told her we might have to use logical consequences and ground her if she ever did the same kind of thing again.

The way Kim remembers it, I used logical consequences in less than the ideal textbook fashion—it sounded like a threat to her—but at any rate it worked. Kim went upstairs to her room crying and was never guilty of the infraction again. Throughout high school any conflicts she had with us were settled without resorting to logical consequences. Sometimes, however, she would tease me about needing some logical consequences for failing to do my usual chores around the house.

Jeff, our older son, never responded well to logical consequences (or any other kind for that matter). As I mentioned in earlier chapters, we tried just about everything to get him to cooperate on curfew, but nothing worked very well.

Jeff and I did have some interesting conflict-resolution sessions though. We negotiated curfew, maintaining the yard, and taking the garbage cans out to the curb for pick up once a week. I was reasonable (or so I thought) while Jeff was shrewd. We would work something out, but the solution was only temporary. Soon we would be right back at the negotiating table. As I would seek new resolutions to old conflicts, Jeff would sell me his point of view with the skill of a carnival pitchman.

While conflict with Jeff never seemed to end, I still feel our negotiation sessions did create some kind of communication channel. Usually, we could talk, except for the night of the Battle at Kitchen Sink (see chapter 7).

With Todd, our younger son, who is now 18, resolving conflicts and using logical consequences worked quite a bit better. As I've mentioned, Todd is not one for long, drawn-out conversations, particularly when conflict or disagreement is involved. If a logical consequence had to be invoked, he would accept it matter-of-factly. "Logical consequences are a fair way to work it out," he says. "When you're a teenager you can't have everything your own way and logical consequences are a good compromise."

Key Attitude #9: Fairness

As a parent I like to think "I'm trying to be fair." But *fairness* is an attitude that is especially foreign to human nature. It's much easier to be fair to myself as I dismiss my teenagers' needs as unreasonable or immature. I have so many feelings of my own that I fail to actively listen for theirs. I try to send an "I" message, but they only hear "you blew it."

But I push on, trying to work out conflicts and find solutions that are fair to everyone. I am willing to give at some points, and to lose when I can see I am wrong, misinformed, or being proud or stubborn. But there are still those times when I can't give, and my teenager isn't about to give either. Those are the sticky times. Somebody has to call the shots. You can't spend your lives negotiating a six-point plan.

Because I am trying to parent from a Christian perspective, it is encouraging to remember that I and my teenagers are in this thing together—in the Lord. Children are to obey and respect their parents *in the Lord*. Parents are to bring children up in the nurture and admonition *of the Lord*.

God, the ultimate authority, has placed me in authority over my children. I am in charge, not my teenagers. I have "power," but if I am wise, I realize my power is limited and growing more so every day. I do not equate my authority with power, rather I balance my authority with my responsibility as a parent. As I deparent authoritatively I have authority, but I work at transferring more and more responsibility to my teenager so he or she can become mature and responsible.

My teenagers are just as responsible for their choices as I am. If they choose to put their desires ahead of everyone else's, they are saying they want freedom without responsibility. When that happens, nobody wins. Logical consequences may come into play, and the deparenting process is temporarily on hold. I would like to see my teenager handle curfew, garbage cans, dating, driving, money, etc. with no problem. But there are those times when he is not ready. So it's back to square one temporarily. I am not interested in punishment, I am interested in seeing my teenagers grow and become more responsible while I deparent and become less responsible for nursing them along or bailing them out.

All of this is not easy. Come to think of it, nobody ever said it would be. And I didn't ask for Paul's marching orders, but there they are in Ephesians 6:4. I am not to work out my differences with my teenagers so I always win while they always lose and grow more and more resentful. I am to help them grow and mature, as I train them in an atmosphere of give-and-take, where I do more than just try to be fair, and when I am wrong I admit it.

And I have been wrong my share of the time. From what I hear teenagers saying about their parents, I have a lot of company. Parenting teenagers might not be the toughest job in the world, but it's got to rank right up there with putting out oil-well fires, disarming bombs, or trying to negotiate peace at prison riots. About all I can do is trust. I have to trust myself to do the best I can. I have to trust my teenager to cooperate and above all, I have to trust God. That's a lot of trust, and in chapter 10 we'll take a closer look at how it's done.

FOR THOUGHT, DISCUSSION, AND ACTION

1. On a scale of 1 to 10 (10 being excellent) rate yourself on how fair you are in disciplining and controlling your teenager. Then sit down and ask your teenager how he would rate you.

2. Have you ever used the "I" message as part of communicating with your teenager? Start listening to conversations in your home and how often a "you" message is sent by one person to another. Check your own use of "you" messages and try to start changing them to "I" messages when you face a problem or conflict that must be resolved.

3. Read Hebrews 12:5-11. What does this passage tell you about how God sees His relationship to the Christian? What does this passage tell you about how you should see your relationship to your teenager?

4. James 3:17 is loaded with ideas for the authoritative parent to use with his teenagers when resolving conflicts and working out logical consequences. See especially *The Living Bible, Para-*

phrased and list the many attributes of the "wisdom that comes from heaven." Which attributes are you using and which could you use more often? See also Romans 12:9–11 for a comparative study.

5. How does the concept of conflict resolution strike you?
   a. I'm already using it.
   b. It sounds a little risky to me—too permissive.
   c. I think I will try it.
6. Have you ever used logical consequences? Do you believe you have done it correctly or as just another form of punishment? Rate yourself on the following key points regarding use of logical consequences (Mark each question *Yes, No,* or *Sometimes*):

_____ a. I use logical consequences as a disciplinary tool.

_____ b. I use logical consequences as a weapon or a threat.

_____ c. I try to work out logical consequences with my teenager beforehand.

_____ d. I make sure both of us know all the ground rules.

_____ e. I let my teenager decide what the logical consequences will be.

_____ f. I sometimes use logical consequences as a punishment and decide what they will be after my teenager breaks a rule or fails in some other responsibility.

_____ g. When a rule is broken or a responsibility is unmet and logical consequences are in order, I follow through and enforce the consequence every time.

10.

Deparenting Takes a Lot of Trust

"Please trust me. I am a big girl and can take care of myself"
(Camille, 18).

HOW MUCH DO YOU trust your teenager? According to my survey of junior-high, high-school, and college-age young people, many parents would claim, "quite a bit." When I asked several hundred teenagers, "How could you get your parents to trust you more?" over 50 percent of them answered: "They trust me enough." Another 30 percent, however, believed they could get their parents to trust them more if they would: "Act more responsibly."

The issue of acting responsibly seems to be behind a lot of parental concerns about trust. Even though many teenagers will claim their parents "trust" them, they still admit to numerous areas of tension and friction.

For example, one question on my questionnaire was "My parents have not trusted me as much as I would have liked concerning. . . ." Here are just a few of hundreds of answers given by high-school and college students: use of the house . . . living on my own, taking care of myself . . . being alone with girlfriend . . . whereabouts and who with . . . friends, going out . . . making mature decisions . . . having kids over while they're not home . . . what I say, they think I'm lying sometimes . . . things I do when I go out . . . common sense . . . eating (afraid I'll starve myself) . . . sex . . . partying and staying out . . . using the car.

"You Were Cruising for *Six* Hours?"

The list goes on and on, but you get the idea. Parents may say they trust their teenagers, but they still worry about how they actually function when on their own, with no parent around. There are many parents who are not always sure their son or daughter will "act responsibly." And, the problem doesn't lie only with younger adolescents in junior high or high school. I found a great deal of it at the college level as well.

When asked what she would like her parents to know about her, Jan, a 19-year-old freshman, said: "I would like to tell them they have raised a reasonable, intelligent, and responsible kid. I know they still have control over me because I live under their roof, but I just ask that they consider my point of view and trust me in the decisions I make regarding the future."

Elizabeth, 18, a university freshman, put it a little more succinctly: "Mom, please let go of me a little more."

Lisa, 18 and a college freshman, says her parents "always trusted me," but she recalls: "When I used to go out, back home, I'd come home and they'd say, 'Oh, what did you do?' Or, 'Where did you go last night?' If they knew I had been gone from like six to twelve, and if I said, 'We went cruising or just to so-and-so's house' they would say, 'You were cruising for *six hours?* Wait, no you weren't, something else happened you're not telling us.' It got down to where I started jotting down minutes as I was driving down the boulevard, you know, 'We stopped for a Coke at 10:45,' it got down to that. But it got ridiculous after awhile. I guess they thought that cruising and messing around you might meet some weirdo or something. I don't know."

Jeanine, a 16-year-old junior in high school, still remembers the time her dad checked on her and her 15-year-old sister as the two sat talking in the park. "My dad comes down to the park in his car and asks us if we want to go for some ice cream. He just had ice cream an hour before! And he's sitting there looking around, trying to see who was out there with us. It was funny to watch him trying to scope something out, and there was nothing there but me and my sister."

If you can't quite identify with any of the scenes described above, you can probably fill in with one of your own. When it comes to trust and letting go, every parent has moments when the questions come: "Where are they? Are they okay? What are they doing? I hope they're not in trouble." Call it mistrust, being anxious, worry—it's all a part of the process of deparenting.

We have already seen in chapter 3 how the deparenting process should speed up as children become teenagers. The "river" of Negotiable Responsibility widens out to include all kinds of problem areas, many of which are the same bones of contention listed by teenagers who want their parents to trust them more: using the car, being with friends, going out, spending money, dating, making decisions, etc. (see chart below).

Mindy's Five-Year Plan

The deparenting process is a coin with two distinct sides. On one side the teenager wants more freedom and independence. On the other, parents want their teenager to take more responsibility.

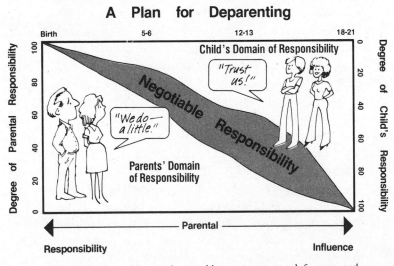

Trust—or the lack of it—can be a problem as teenagers ask for more and more freedom.

When Gary Hess' two daughters reached adolescence, he worked out a plan to give them more trust as they took on more responsibility. In turn, they would feel more freedom and independence, at least that's what Gary and his wife Lola hoped.

For example, when Mindy Hess had her thirteenth birthday, Gary and Lola sat down with their daughter and explained:

"Now that you're a teenager, we know there will be a lot of things you'll be wanting to do, and we want to turn them over to you as we think you're ready. Some things will be turned over right now or in a short time. Other things we'll have to negotiate as we go along. At 18 you may want to choose to go to college or move out and get a job; between now and then our goal is to really help you become independent and responsible."

Gary then mentioned some of the key issues and areas that he and Lola knew were of concern to Mindy, as well as to them: care of her room, curfew, bedtime, studies, and homework. Down the road there would be things like dating, a driver's license, owning a car, and financial independence.

Gary remembers that schoolwork was not exactly something new for Mindy at 13, but what he and Lola were concerned about as she began junior high was that she would always "do her best."

Gary then added, "These are some of the areas that we'll all be working on in the next five years. When we'll work on each one, we're not sure. We'll take them as you're ready and as they come, and there will probably be some we didn't talk about tonight."

One thing Mindy's parents turned over to her on the spot was care of her own room. It had been a real bone of contention, that had caused continual nagging, especially by Mom. "From 13 on," Gary said, "your room is your responsibility. Mom will not clean it up for you or pick up your dirty clothes. You have to get your own clothes out to the laundry room or Mom will not worry about washing them. You're on your own!"

Clothes, Budgets, and Boyfriends

Mindy was quite happy with the new room arrangement, until the morning she had no clean clothes for school because she had forgotten to get her laundry to Mom for washing and ironing. So, Mindy had to pick an outfit out of the wrinkled piles in her room and iron it herself. All this took some time, and she was late to school in the bargain. There were tears, dirty looks and wails of remorse and embarrassment, but Gary and Lola hung tough and let "logical consequences"[1] teach Mindy that her room was indeed her responsibility.

"Let's get you to school," Gary told her, "and tonight we'll talk about it." That night Gary, Lola, and Mindy went over the Conflict Resolution Process described in chapter 9. Mindy's complaint was that it was hard to always get her dirty clothes clear out to the clothes hamper in the laundry room. The new solution for Mindy: putting a clothes hamper in her room so she could keep her clothes picked up. She was still responsible, however, for getting the clothes to Lola for washing each week.

Other new challenges soon arrived. In a few months Mindy started refusing to wear clothes Lola would buy for her. She wanted to choose her own. After running the problem through the Conflict Resolution Process, Gary and Lola put Mindy on her own clothes budget of twenty-five dollars a month (a reasonable sum at that period of inflationary history). Mindy enjoyed her new responsibility—so much so that she soon was overspending at an alarming rate. So, it was back to the negotiating table to resolve the problem. The new solution: Mindy could spend in advance no more than three months of her allowance (seventy-five dollars). Then she would have to wait until new money was available.

Next came Mindy's first boyfriend, with the interesting complication that neither Mindy nor her friend was old enough to drive. The "conflict" in this case was that the youngsters needed to be driven to their dates—for example, the movies. In typical teenage fashion, they seldom planned very far ahead. Friday or Saturday night would come and they would need a ride just about the time Gary and Lola were leaving for somewhere.

Picking them up was also a problem. The boy's parents were trying to help with transportation, too, but they also had engagements and could not always change plans at the last minute. Negotiations with Mindy established her responsibility to let Gary and Lola know several days ahead what her plans were, so rides could be worked out.

Some Principles for Deparenting

The above examples with Mindy are not what most parents would call earthshaking crises. But they all demonstrate how a plan for deparenting can actually work. Here are important principles to keep in mind:

1. Let the teenager know you want to give him or her more freedom and independence and you will be happy to do so in the form of "negotiating responsibilities." Then, as your teenager tries the normal questions, challenges, and tests to expand his or her domain of personal freedom, you have a structure for dealing with it.

2. Make trust an automatic part of the entire process. You can't "negotiate responsibility" without using trust. Once you give the responsibility (and the freedom), it's up to you to trust your teenager to follow through.

3. If the negotiated responsibility is a sensitive one—dating, for example—talk about it with your teenager. Share your concerns about certain types of friends and acquaintances, the possible dangers, etc. Let your teenager know that you really want to give more freedom, but you need to know that he or she is working on responsibility. If there is a more serious kind of disagreement and some kind of communication logjam, bring the "I" message into play and work the Conflict Resolution Process. Keep things out on the negotiating table and always give your teenager the benefit of the doubt.

4. Keep logical consequences handy, but use them sparingly. As the authoritative parent you are in charge, but open to give-and-take and all the challenges and tests your teenager will throw at you. As you negotiate responsibilities, don't start out by saying, "Now if you don't do this right, it will mean the following consequences will be in force."

First, set up the area of freedom/responsibility. Then try it out and see what happens. If there is a problem, try resolving it with the Conflict Resolution Process. If the problem persists, *then* talk about logical consequences. Point out, "Look, I want to trust you, but this hasn't been working. What do you think is a fair consequence if you don't hold up your end and your responsibilities?"

Is all this a lot of trouble? Of course it's a lot of trouble. But as the mechanic in the oil-filter ad on TV puts it, "You can pay now or you can pay later." Using the deparenting plan—along with active listening, "I" messages, and the Conflict Resolution Process—is the way you pay now with proper maintenance to head off trouble down the line. That's the idea behind putting clean filters in an engine. If you come at it with no plan, and no basis for communication and trust, the trouble comes later and you pay with bigger headaches, more hassles, and more relationships that need overhauling, just like engines that haven't had proper filter care.

With our kids, I didn't have the benefit of Gary's complete deparenting plan. I sort of winged it by using things I read or heard along with a certain amount of common sense, which sometimes fluctuated with my moods and energy. I used some of the techniques, such as active listening and the "I" message, but I can see that the missing element was communicating to Kim, Jeff, and Todd at 13 or even 12 that we wanted to guide and develop them instead of control them.

With Jeff in particular this might have helped make our conflict resolution sessions more of an adventure in joint problem-solving rather than our own version of the popular song that talks about knowing when to hold, fold, walk away, or run. Or, to put it in an athletic metaphor, I could have used a strategy that would have helped me avoid being constantly on the defensive, always playing "catch up."

But What Happens When They "Really Blow It"?

There is no guarantee that the deparenting plan described above will work flawlessly. In fact, you can be practically certain your teenager will not perform flawlessly, just as you didn't for your parents. Teenagers blow it. They sometimes abuse parental trust. What then?

Some parents make a critical mistake. They remove all trust by generalizing from one violation or mistake that everything the teenager does is suspect.

Sue, a college junior, remembers her problems when she blew it back in high school:

"Of course my parents had reason not to trust me. I wasn't a real bad girl, but at 15 I started going around with this bum group of people. Once I went to a party and everyone got busted. I had been in this pool hall most of the night because I didn't want to go to this party where there was drinking. But I finally agreed to go, and just as I got to the party the cops came. I got picked up for breaking curfew, and the rest got picked up for being drunk.

"We went to the jailhouse. It was one of the most degrading things that ever happened to me. Going to the jailhouse and being stripped completely of all your clothes was the most degrading thing. They were looking for drugs, I guess. I had told my parents I was going to a movie. Finally, at 4 A.M. my dad came to the jail to pick me up, and I got in a lot of trouble. I didn't get to explain my side at all, and I already felt so bad.

"After that, Mom and Dad never quit using it against me, and to this day there are things I've done wrong that Mom will bring up. And the hardest part is that I wanted them to trust me and see that even if I made a mistake, I still had enough going for me that I could figure things out. If they could have just talked to me and let me discuss it and find out, 'What happened?' I probably would have never gotten into trouble again. And when they would bring up my past, it would really hurt. In 1 Corinthians 13 it talks about love does not remember things that were done wrong, but it doesn't seem like that's what happens in so many families."

Mike, a college sophomore, has the same story, but his terse comment on a questionnaire does not fill in details: "They trusted me until I blew it, and then they held it over my head."

Michelle, 15, adds: "What frustrates me is my dad doesn't trust me. There's no trust at all. And then he says, 'Well, prove I can trust you.' And there's no way 'cause I'm at school half the time. I come home, I eat dinner, and go to sleep. I don't spend any time with him, and he doesn't spend any time with me . . . we have no communication . . . how am I supposed to prove my trust . . . how can I prove it to him?''

The Fallacy of "Earn My Trust"

The above comments reveal the many problems involved in giving or removing trust. Lack of communication, lack of forgiveness, a vengeful attitude, no understanding, nobody listening are all there, while trust is absent. When parents say, "Earn my trust" or "Prove you can be trusted" they put their teenager—and themselves—in a bind. The vicious cycle works like this:

The teenager blows it. He breaks a rule, makes a mistake, does something irresponsible, etc. The parent says, "No more trust until you prove you can be trusted." But as Michelle asks, how can the teenager prove he's worthy of something he isn't being given? The basic attitude behind the "prove I can trust you" stance is one of distrust. Note, too, Sue's opening words in her story: "My parents had reason not to trust me." Her parents kept her on a chronic guilt trip by not forgiving her and starting over by trusting again.

Perhaps trust is like forgiveness. It needs to be given again and again. Sue is right. First Corinthians 13 says, "Love . . . keeps no record of wrongs . . . It always protects, always trusts, always perseveres" (vv. 5, 7, NIV). I tell parenting classes and seminars one basic thing about trusting teenagers. You might as well; you don't have any other reasonable choice. Distrust simply breeds more distrust, but if you keep trusting your teenager, sooner or later the message will get through.

Am I saying a parent should be a naïve pushover? Hardly. Parents should never let a teenager get away with the same flaunting of rules or continued promiscuous behavior without confronting the situation. But it's *how* you confront the problem that counts, and I doubt that laying down the ''prove I can trust you'' gauntlet really helps. Why even talk about ''trust'' per se? Talk about the problem and how to resolve it.

If the teenager is really offbase, you may have to take a certain privilege or behavior out of the Negotiable Responsibility area for awhile. If the teenager wants to scream, ''Distrust!'' so be it, but it's not a question of trust or distrust. It's a question of working together to develop responsibility in your son or daughter. Keep communication going and as soon as possible reopen negotiation and give your teenager a new shot at it.

Key Attitude #10: Trust

All of the above is nice theory, but how does it translate into developing the much-needed attitude of real *trust* while in the heat of the deparenting battle?

First, you have to trust yourself. You may have a full-blown strategy for deparenting, or you may be basically winging it with not much more going for you than common sense. What counts is having confidence in your love for your kids and your desire to do the best job you can. Family counselor Barbara Levy, appearing on a segment of the ''Good Morning, America!'' television broadcast with David Hartman, stressed that a primary need in teenagers is for parents who care enough to draw the line ''. . . to say it clearly—'I don't like it, I don't want you to do that.' It says to them I love you very much and I care about your life.''

Hartman then asked Levy if there was any way to know if you are being ''a terrific, perfect parent.'' She replied: ''There is no such thing. In the history of the world, I don't think anyone has done it exactly right, but we can try.''[2]

Second, you trust your teenager. If you can trust yourself and your basic instincts, you gain the confidence and security to trust your kids. Teenagers who felt loved and trusted put remarks like the following on their questionnaires:

"Dad, Mom, you're doing a great job. I love you both; look how we've turned out and that should show you how you've done in raising us!" (Brian, 19).

"You have done a great job—I appreciate the openness, the honesty, the faith, and the love that you have taught me—thanks!" (Peggy, a college freshman).

"Keep up the good work!" (Cathy, 19).

"I look up to them and they set an example that I follow. They are the ones to whom I turn and I think very highly of both. I respect them and they respect me and in this way we relate to one another" (Paula, 18).

Trusting yourself and trusting your teenager only happen in direct proportion to how much you trust God. Our heavenly Father is our ultimate model. We, His children, make mistakes and disappoint Him, but He continues to trust us, and He yearns to have us trust Him in return. Job, who raised a few teenagers himself, knew the secret. When all the lights seemed to go out at the end of his tunnel, Job was still able to say: "Though he slay me, yet will I trust in him" (Job 13:15, KJV).

Jackie and I got just a taste of this kind of trusting after Jeff had been out of high school for a year. He was making good money as an apprentice electrician, and he announced that he wanted to move out of the house and get on his own. He and three buddies had plans to rent a large house just down the road a few miles. I had seen Jeff's departure coming and was ambivalent. Jeff needed to get out, but I felt uneasy about his state of mind which at that time could have been described as controlled hostility. Jackie didn't like the idea at all. To put it in deparenting-plan terminology, she saw Jeff's desire to move out as a rejection of his parents rather than stepping out of the nest into independence and total responsibility.

The first few weeks after Jeff moved out were especially hard for Jackie. The phone kept ringing and the callers kept asking for Jeff. She would say, "He isn't in." She could not bring herself to utter the words, "He has moved out. Would you like his new number?"

For nineteen years we had done our best with trusting—and retrusting—Jeff, but now we moved into a new dimension. For the first time he was really gone, on his own, setting his own curfew, and choosing to attend or not attend church. We were quite sure it was the latter because church had bored him most of the time during junior high and high school.

So, we settled in to live with a less-than-perfect record in deparenting (not exactly a new condition). Kim had married a fine Christian fellow and they had moved away. Todd was working his way through the classic teenage fluctuations—from chipper and enthusiastic to growly and grumpy to silent depression—often all in one day and sometimes several times a day. But he was *with* us in body and spirit (as long as his mother could use her magic fingers on the bottom of his basketball-worn feet).

But Jeff had not turned out like the deparenting manual said he would. We had prayed constantly for him when he lived at home. Now we prayed harder and committed him anew to the Lord. Our door remained open to him and he'd drop by frequently—to introduce a new girlfriend or just "kick back" and have a TV show or two with popcorn. We didn't talk much with him about "life with the guys," but we trusted and trusted some more as we wondered what God had in mind for Jeff.

Jackie wept her way through *Parents in Pain,* John White's excellent work for families with erstwhile teenagers. I wasn't quite ready for *Parents in Pain,* but I was a parent who pondered. With my choleric/melancholy penchant for perfection, I see-sawed between guilt and second-guessing myself all the way over to "I tried everything—my son doesn't just march to a different drummer, he has his own private band."

The classic "trust" passages of Scripture haunted the hallways of our minds:

"Trust in the Lord with all thine heart; and lean not unto thine own understanding. In all thy ways acknowledge him and he shall direct thy paths" (Prov. 3:5,6, KJV). "Commit thy way unto the Lord; trust also in him; and he shall bring it to pass" (Ps. 37:5, KJV).

Some verses in the first chapter of James were particularly disturbing. If I lack wisdom I should ask God who will give it generously without finding fault, but I must ask in faith and not waver. If I waver, I'm like a wave of the sea, driven and tossed. I'm a double-minded man, unstable in all my ways, and I can't expect to receive anything from the Lord. (See James 1:5–8.)

Ouch. Had James ever had teenagers? I had wavered frequently as I tried to authoritatively nurture my children in the Lord. But maybe that is what trust is all about—not being sure, but still having confidence God is in this thing someplace and He *will* come through. Maybe trusting God is like trusting your teenager. You might as well—you really don't have a good alternative.

FOR THOUGHT, DISCUSSION, AND ACTION

1. How would you answer the question, "How much do you trust your teenager?" Are there areas of tension and doubt? If so, have you ever asked your teenager to work through these with you as you try to deparent? Send some "I" messages designed to simply reveal your vulnerability and need for support—in prayer, in communicating and in trying to understand. Remind your teenager that a lot of things are new ground for you, and it's not easy to walk where you haven't walked before.

2. Do you have a plan or strategy for deparenting such as the one used by Gary Hess with his daughter Mindy (see pages 166 to 169)? How would something like this work with you and your teenager? What would happen if you went over parts of this chapter with your teenager and entered into a deparenting agreement? Are you ready to spend the time and effort?

3. Has your teenager ever blown it? Do you hold it over his head, or maybe keep it in a hidden agenda? If so, how is this helping your relationship?

4. Do you agree or disagree with the idea: "You might as well trust your teenager—you don't have a reasonable alternative"? Is

trust something earned or given freely as God gives grace? Can a parent be too trusting? Under what circumstances?

5. Do a study on trust in your study Bible or concordance. Then complete the following: ''Trusting God concerning my teenager is something I do when. . . .''

Conclusion
_____

What Teenagers
Really Need

CONCLUSIONS TO BOOKS usually attempt to wrap things up
and tidy up loose ends. I'll try to do both. You may want to know
how Jeff's story came out. Or you may be wondering when I'm
going to get to the good parts, like what to do about: dating and
sex, living-together arrangements, homosexuality, drugs, alcohol, unwanted pregnancies, refusal to go to church, delinquency,
runaways, peer pressure, single parenting of teenagers, teenage
suicide, grand theft auto, and how to get them to love their youth
group.

I do not intend to make light of these and many other problems
that are breaking parents' hearts throughout the world. Many excellent books have been written on all these topics, and I have tried
to list some of them in Appendix 2, "Resources for Parents." I
like to think, however, that I have covered a lot of the problems,
but in a different way. By stressing attitudes and relationships, I
tried to move back a notch or two to where the problems with sex,
drugs, alcohol, etc. usually start.

After parenting three kids of my own, and talking to a lot of
them I didn't parent, I am convinced that the *relationship* between
parent and child is primary. Whatever happens between you and
your teenager is commentary on the kind of *attitudes* you are
bringing to that relationship.

Try Talking about Attitudes

Reading and thinking about attitudes is helpful. "Yes," most of us can say, "I really should be more understanding, respectful, accepting, thoughtful, forgiving, fair, and trusting. Got to remember to work on those." There is an old story about a man who slept through most of the pastor's sermon, and as the final "amens" were dying away, he opened one eye and asked his wife, "Is the sermon done?" She answered, "The sermon is finished, it is yet to be *done*."

If you want to live life in a little faster lane, try talking with (not to) your teenager about your attitudes and how you can make specific changes for the better. Yes, I know, it's your teenager who has some attitudes that need changing. That's probably true, but we're assuming that you do have a fault or two that needs a bit of work. Besides, didn't Jesus say something about not worrying about splinters in the eyes of others when you have enough logs to contend with in your own?

Following are some "conversation starter" questions you may be able to use with your teenager. You may not feel you can use them all, due to your son's or daughter's ages, current state of mind, or the general emotional climate between the two of you right now. And you may want to modify some of the questions or ask different ones. The important thing is to try to make the conversation as relaxed as possible.

One possible beginning could be: "I've been reading this book, *What Teenagers Wish Their Parents Knew about Kids,* and I'd like to have you tell me how I could improve on some of my attitudes."

Your teenager is quite likely to respond in one of two ways—with incredulity or suspicion. He may very possibly think this is a "setup" so you can trap him and do some criticizing of *his* attitudes. And, indeed, some of your teenager's answers to these questions may put you on the defensive; they may even put you on the *offensive*. But it's crucial that you keep the pressure on yourself and allow your teenager to be honest and open. Caution: don't try this if you feel at all tense, frustrated, or tired. And don't try all ten areas at once. Following are ideas for talking about understanding and respect. Suggestions for discussing the other eight attitudes (letting go, acceptance, thoughtfulness, perseverance, forgiveness, self-control, fairness, trust) can be found in Appendix 1, "Talking about Attitudes" (page 193).

Understanding

Do I try to understand you enough? Do you feel I always care about your problems, pressures, and struggles? What could I do that would help me understand you better? What can I say that would help you understand me better?

Respect

Do you feel I have respect for you as a person? Do you see me treating other adults with more respect than I treat you? If so, what do I do that tells you that? What would you like me to do to show you I respect you?

Using the above questions with your teenager can range all the way from rewarding and gratifying to not too helpful. The whole idea may work better with one teenager than another. It may take several tries before your son or daughter believes you really want to change. Remember, too, that your teenager's attitude may be such that you can't get through. Sometimes the walls grow high and thick. If so, I understand; I've been there.

"I Wanted to Do My Thing . . ."

In chapter 10 you got a father's-eye view of his 19-year-old son moving out under less than perfect circumstances. To help conclude this discussion of what teenagers wish parents could know, I asked Jeff to put some thoughts on tape, about why he left and what happened after that. Some of what follows is easy to share; some of it makes me realize I missed some other important parental attitudes—like humility. Anyway, here's Jeff, with occasional station breaks by "Big Christian Father," now trimmed down to size.

"When I moved out I felt a lot of relief and excitement. I could finally do pretty much as I pleased. I could come home from work, and if someone called at 10 o'clock at night and wanted to do something, I could just go. If Rex (one of my housemates) and I wanted to have dates over for a Bar-B-Q, we did that. If I wanted to have a few beers in the fridge, I did that . . . it was no big deal.

"After I moved out in May, I met a girl and we started going together. She was fun, and it was laugh, laugh, laugh all summer long.

"I could sleep in on Sundays, and I didn't really care about going to church. I was happy, I was having a lot of laughs. And I was advancing at work, plus getting a lot of electrical jobs on the side. Lots of good things were going for me."

Our "prodigal" was out there having a good time, but unlike the young man in Luke 15, he was doing it on his own tab. Meanwhile, his mother and I made a pleasant discovery. Because he was "out of our hands" it was easier to pray and trust him to God's hands. And, we actually had more peace without the constant irritations and tensions that plagued us while he lived at home.

"Toward the end of summer, my girlfriend and I broke up. Then some of the guys living at our place began to move out. Finally, it was just Rex and I. I was paying four hundred dollars to five hundred dollars a month in bills, plus going out a lot.

"As we got into the fall, I started spending a lot more time by myself. I had more time to think, but being alone bothered me. When I'd get down, I'd have to get out of there. I'd go four-wheelin' in the truck I'd bought, or I'd ride my dirt bike, or I'd call up a girl, or I'd call up my friends. I had to be doing something with somebody. I kept cruisin' through.

"I also did a lot of thinking about why I'd moved away from home. The main reason was I didn't want any more pressure from my parents. I wanted to do my thing. I thought I was big enough and old enough to handle life on my own. I didn't really enjoy being around Mom and Dad—we argued a lot, and it seemed that I was always having to give a detailed description of what I was doing, why I was doing it, and when I was doing it, and when I would be home.

"But after seven or eight months of freedom and fun, the novelty was wearing off. I started feeling lonely. I started thinking about Mom and Dad more and maybe living at home hadn't really been that bad after all. So, I went and talked with them about moving back in, but I needed to get some things squared away—curfews, for example."

When Jeff asked if he could move back in, my response was fairly positive, but Jackie was ambivalent. Her mother's heart knew she was going to let him move back—it was what we had been praying for—but she feared the hassles and tension would return with him. We had decided, however, that we had hassled curfews with Jeff for the last time.

I told him, "You can have your own room back, and there is no set time for being in. We haven't known how late you were out for the last eight months, so why should we worry about it now?" Jeff looked surprised—but quite pleased.

So our prodigal moved back home in March. We didn't kill the fatted calf, but the price was right on his room—not anywhere near half what he had been paying at the other place.

"After I moved back home, I started going to church again. I could see that no matter what I had bought or what I did, it would only satisfy temporarily. I'm not sure why I started thinking more about God, but I did. All the time I had been away from home I knew God was there. I even prayed once in awhile, but I didn't make it a big priority.

"I noticed I was getting sick and tired of going to work and

listening to all of the filthy talk and putting up with a lot of the corruption and cutting corners. I didn't have the cleanest mouth in the world myself, and I really worked on shaping that up. For some reason I started trying to keep things clean and be honest."

I wish I could report that I "finally got through to Jeff for Jesus." But while our relationship was cordial, I didn't feel any openings to talk about spiritual matters. So, I waited and watched, not really aware of what he was thinking. . . .

"I could see that you can't get satisfaction out of things or even friends. I guess I saw myself looking more and more toward God. Then I met Debbi—actually I remet her; I had known her almost all my life, and we had gone to school together. I guess I was right in the middle of recommitting my life to God, and she helped me get squared away. She showed me that you can be a Christian without being uptight and stiff. Her faith was down to earth and that impressed me.

"Along with everything else, I started thinking about going to college. I was burned out on working. Maybe it was like Dad had been telling me: 'Try college and see where it goes. You can always go back to electrical work.' Now the idea made sense. I applied late to a Christian liberal-arts school and got accepted just before applications for the term closed."

Jackie and I were pleased by Jeff's decision to go to college, but I worried about how he would handle liberal-arts courses after majoring in basketball and dating in high school. He was bright enough, but hitting the books was foreign territory. And he did struggle—especially the first semester—but he hung in there. He even passed Old Testament Survey, an accomplishment somewhat tantamount to crossing the Red Sea. More important, however, he crossed some important territory of his own.

"I think I've grown up a lot after a year in college. Before I moved back home I never gave God a chance to do what He can

do. I used to just turn off to all that. God? What can He do? Come on, that's just coincidence when good things happen. I realize more and more now that as I let Him do more things in my life that more and more He replaces the things that didn't satisfy me.

"When I look back to high school I always felt I never could relate to Mom and Dad, so why should I stay there. I didn't feel at home. I didn't feel like they understood anything I said. They had their opinions on how they felt about things, and while they would hear me out, I still knew how they felt in the back of their minds. They might say, 'Okay, go ahead and do this or do that,' but I knew that in some cases they were reluctant and really felt differently. It was kind of like they half-way tried to understand me.

"I realize now how special parents are, and what kind of parents I do have compared to a lot of others. After I started letting God handle my life, I hardly ever got mad anymore. I always like to listen to other people now and what their side is rather than be stubborn. I feel like I've really changed there."

Yes, Jeff, you have really changed—and so have your mother and I.

"I never thought God would be the most important thing in my life, but I can't wait to learn more about what He can do. At school I took Old Testament and New Testament courses, and I can see I'm really a rookie. I've gone to church all my life, but I never listened. I've come a ways, and I still have a ways to go. I'm thinking about being a missionary, one way or another. Who knows? Right now I'm studying to be a teacher because I think it's rewarding to help kids and be an influence.

"I look at life a lot differently now than I used to. I'm more concerned for others and their lives and where their heads are. I used to always think about me and what I could do to better myself. I've also realized that I still have a lot of growing up to do, which I really didn't think was true before I went to college. I realize there are some areas God and I have to work on and that takes time."

Go, God, Go!

Jeff's tape said a lot more, but that was the gist of it. There are several responses his parents could make:

a. The Lord does answer prayer.
b. God's grace is boundless, constant—and amazing.
c. God works through us, around us, and sometimes, in spite of us.
d. As Ziggy* said, while gazing into a glorious sunset: "Go, God!"

I like all of the above, especially Ziggy's enthusiasm for what God can do. I appreciate Jeff's comment about having some things to work on and how it will all take time. The ball game is a long way from the bottom of the ninth. God isn't finished with *any* of us *yet*. But now that the deparenting is almost over, I'm grateful God trusted us with teenagers. We had some good times, some "normal" times, and a few times when I would have sold them all at three for a nickel. But I wouldn't trade any of them for the world.

So, thank you, Kim, Jeff, and Todd, for putting your mom and me through Deparenting University. Now that we are almost ready for our diplomas, we have the message. And it's the same message that all those other teenagers I surveyed are trying to send their folks. Teenagers aren't really asking their parents to be primarily brilliant, skilled, or even "effective." They aren't, first and foremost, wishing we were capable, competent, and organized. And the top of their priority list doesn't even feature parents who are powerful, potent, and always prepared.

All these things are good, but they are the cart, not the horse. The teenagers I have lived with, and the ones I surveyed, all told me the same thing in different ways. They are looking *first of all*

---

*By "Ziggy" I refer, of course, to the lovable little cartoon character who suffers life's slings and arrows in a style familiar to many parents.

for attitudes that tell them they are really wanted, they are valued and cherished, and they are trusted as capable and competent.

Listen once more to the youthful witnesses from my survey travels as they testify concerning their needs. From the Amys, the Chips, the Sallys, the Cyndis, the Donnas, the Claudias, the Johns, the Steves, the Daves, come these pleas:

"Don't be ashamed of me, help me."

"Trust me, let me learn things for myself. . . ."

"Let me live my own life."

"Learn to notice when I hurt . . . even though I'm great at holding it in."

"Be nice to me."

"Believe in me."

"Accept me for what I am."

"Be concerned . . . suggest things to me, but don't force me."

Yes, there is a strong note of "me" and "I" in these remarks. Can't these kids think of anyone but themselves? Yes, and no. They are making that rite of passage into adulthood. It's scary territory, and when you're even a little bit scared, it's natural to look around for life jackets labeled "self-preservation." ·

What teenagers wish parents knew about kids is that even "big kids" need parents with attitudes that show understanding, respect, and willingness to let go. They kind of like it when parents are thoughtful, when they listen, and maybe most of all—when they forgive. And they don't mind parental authority, really, not as long as it's controlled, fair, and trusting.

In short, teenagers need love. I haven't used that expression a lot in this book because it is so easy to corrupt it with clichés. When you think about it, L-O-V-E is a rather inadequate arrangement of four letters to say something quite indescribable in one mere word. St. Paul came as close as any human when he wrote:

"Love is so patient and so kind;
Love never boils with jealousy;
It never boasts, is never puffed with pride;
It does not act with rudeness, or insist upon its rights;

It never gets provoked, it never harbors evil thoughts;
Is never glad when wrong is done,
But always glad when truth prevails;
It bears up under anything,
It exercises faith in everything,
It keeps up hope in everything,
It gives us power to endure in anything.
Love never fails . . . ''

1 Cor. 13:4–8,
WILLIAMS TRANSLATION

Love Never Fails When . . .

Love never fails when it is expressed through actions (clothed in attitudes) like:

. . . not getting upset when your teenagers don't want to be seen with you in public. (understanding)

. . . resisting the urge to steam open that letter addressed to your daughter in an obvious male scrawl. (respect)

. . . acting nonchalant as they leave on their first camping trip without any adults along. (letting go)

. . . letting them try it their way, even when you know it isn't the easiest or the best. (acceptance)

. . . biting a sarcastic reply off the tip of your tongue and saying, "Well, I guess that was an old-fashioned opinion. What do you think should be done?" (thoughtfulness)

. . . being willing to listen to them when you would prefer: the ending of "Sixty Minutes" (or "Donahue"), the last part of the sports page, or the latest issue of *McCalls*. (perseverance)

. . . giving your teenager a smile and a hug and saying, "It's okay . . . I'm glad the car was totaled and not your bod." (forgiveness)

. . . resisting the desire to say, "Look, I feed you, I clothe you, I house you, I car you . . ." and instead saying, "So you feel cutting the lawn once every two weeks is too much. What do you think would be a fair arrangement?" (self-control)

. . . instead of saying, "You are spending me into bank-ruptcy," say, "I am concerned about these bills because they're way beyond the budget we worked out. Let's talk about it." (fairness)

. . . handing *her* boyfriend the keys to *your* car and saying, "Have a great time." (trust)

In these attitudes and many more like them lies the secret of Ephesians 6:4. We have looked at Paul's concise commandment in a lot of different versions of Scripture. If we put them all together, we get a "short course for better parenting":

We parents are not to provoke, irritate, exasperate, scold, nag, goad, or anger our kids. . . .

Instead, we are to instruct, correct, train, discipline, suggest, advise, nurture, admonish, and counsel them in the way the Lord approves.

Paul certainly knows how to portray the authoritative parent. As such I move smoothly through the deparenting process, calmly and coolly transferring more and more responsibility to my teenagers. Fixed firmly in my sights is that glorious ideal: the child who has grown to be a fully functioning, mature adult. And then I will step back and be content. I will have deparented completely, correctly, and authoritatively. I will rest secure in the knowledge that I am revered, venerated, and respected. . . .

I could go on, but you will have to excuse me. Jeff just called from college and tells us he's overdrawn and somebody has to get to the bank to cover a check for $167.83 before closing time.

And there's a note here to call Kim—they just got something in the mail about the mortgage payment on their condo and can I explain it(!).

And Todd just hollered something from the garage about help-ing him with his truck. A delicate adjustment on the engine per-haps? What's that? *He wants me to help lift the truck bed back on the frame?*

Go, God, go.

Notes

Chapter One

1. See F. F. Bruce, *The Epistle to the Ephesians: A Verse by Verse Exposition*, (London: Pickering and Inglis Ltd., 1961), p. 121.
2. See, for example, Bruce Narramore, *Parenting with Love and Limits*, (Grand Rapids: Zondervan Publishing House, 1979), p. 62.
3. As I have talked with other parents, the majority give me the impression that having a successful family time (devotions) with teenagers is not easy. For a list of helpful sources with ideas that you may want to try, see Appendix 2, "Resources for Parents."
4. See James Dobson, *Preparing for Adolescence*, (Santa Ana, CA: Vision House, 1978), chapter 1.

Chapter Two

1. Ross Campbell, *How to Really Love Your Teenager* (Wheaton, IL: Victor Books, 1981), p. 5. Used by permission.
2. Ibid., pp. 10, 11.
3. Ibid., pp. 9, 10.
4. Dorothy Briggs, *Your Child's Self-Esteem* (New York: Dolphin Books, 1975), pp. 3, 4.
5. Taken from *The Sensation of Being Somebody* by Maurice E. Wagner, p. 32 ff. Copyright © 1975 by Maurice E. Wagner. Used by permission of Zondervan Publishing House.
6. Ibid., p. 33.
7. Ibid., p. 34.
8. Ibid., p. 36.
9. Ibid., p. 36.
10. For helpful reading on the three feelings of belongingness, worthiness, and competence, see Maurice Wagner, *The Sensation of Being Somebody*, chapter 4. Wagner's entire book is an excellent study in how to build an adequate self-concept.

Chapter Three

1. Paul Lewis, editor, *Dads Only* 4, no. 11 (Julian, CA, November 1981), p. 2. To subscribe, write to *Dads Only*, P.O. Box 340, Julian CA 92036. Used by permission.

Chapter Four

1. Charles Swindoll, *You and Your Child* (Nashville: Thomas Nelson Publishers, 1977), p. 20.
2. While it is true Dr. Benjamin Spock's first editions of *Baby and Child Care*, his famed manual that guided many parents from the 1940s on, contained many permissive ideas, Spock later "saw the error of his ways" and revised the book in the 1960s and '70s to suggest taking a much firmer hand with children. See the completely revised and updated edition, *Baby and Child Care*, (New York: Pocket Books, 1976).
3. David Keirsey and Marilyn Bates, *Please Understand Me* (Del Mar, CA: Prometheus Nemesis Books, 1978), pp. 4, 5. Used by permission.
4. Fred and Florence Littauer, "Personality Plus Temperaments," Seminar notes, all rights reserved, used by permission.
5. Tim F. LaHaye, *Spirit-Controlled Temperament* (Wheaton, IL: Tyndale House, 1966), *Understanding the Male Temperament* (Old Tappan, NJ: Fleming H. Revell Co., 1977), and *Transformed Temperaments* (Wheaton, IL: Tyndale House, 1971).
6. See also Florence Littauer, *Personality Plus* (Old Tappan, NJ: Fleming H. Revell, 1982), chapters 3–7 and chapter 8–11.

Chapter Five

1. For a complete list, see Thomas Gordon, *Parent Effectiveness Training* (New York: Peter H. Wyden, Inc., 1970), pp. 41–44.
2. See Rex Johnson and Norman Wright, *Building Positive Teen-Parent Relationships* (Eugene, OR: Harvest House Publishers, 1977), pp. 27–36.
3. The actual translation of Proverbs 25:11 is: "A word aptly spoken is like apples of gold in settings of silver" (NIV). The point here is that nothing could be more apt for a parent than to give a word of encouragement to his or her teenager.
4. See Johnson and Wright, *Building Positive Teen-Parent Relationships*, p. 31.
5. Dr. Laurence J. Peter, *Peter's Quotations* (New York: Bantam Books, 1977), p. 551.
6. For more ideas on handling nagging problems and how to quit nagging, see Johnson and Wright, *Building Positive Teen-Parent Relationships*, pp. 33–35.

Chapter Six

1. *To Understand Each Other* by Paul Tournier. Copyright John Knox Press 1972. Used by permission.
2. See, for example, chapter 4, "The Healing Dialogue," Haim Ginott, *Between Parent and Teenager* (New York: Avon Books, 1969). Also see Thomas Gordon, *Parent Effectiveness Training* (New York: Peter H. Wyden, Inc., 1970), chapters 3–7.
3. Jane Norman and Myron Harris, from *The Private Life of the American Teenager*. Copyright © 1981 by Jane Norman and Myron Harris. Reprinted with the permission of Rawson, Wade Publishers, Inc.
4. See Ross Campbell, *How to Really Love Your Teenager* (Wheaton, IL: Victor Books, 1981), pp. 9–11. Used by permission.

Chapter Seven

1. David Mace, "Love, Anger and Intimacy," *Light*, Christian Life Commission of the Southern Baptist Convention, April-May 1980, p. 2.
2. Ibid., p. 2.
3. David Mace, *Love and Anger in Marriage* (Grand Rapids: Zondervan Publishing House, 1982).
4. John's real name is Jeff, but because he and my own son, Jeff, are mentioned at several points in the chapter, I changed his name to avoid possible confusion.
5. *Webster's New Twentieth-Century Dictionary* (New York: Simon and Schuster, 1979), p. 69.
6. See Rex Johnson and Norman Wright, *Building Positive Parent-Teen Relationships* (Eugene, OR: Harvest House, 1977), p. 41.
7. Archibald Hart, *Feeling Free* (Old Tappan, NJ: Fleming H. Revell, 1979), p. 64. Used by permission.
8. Ibid., p. 71.
9. From *Overcoming Frustration and Anger*, by Paul A. Hauck, pp. 43 ff. Copyright © 1974, The Westminster Press, Philadelphia and Sheldon Press, London, England. Used by permission.
10. Archibald Hart, *Feeling Free*, p. 85.
11. Romans 8:26, 27.
12. Archibald Hart, *Feeling Free*, p. 92.
13. Adapted from Phil Sutherland and Norman Rohrer, *Facing Anger* (Minneapolis: Augsburg Publishing House, 1981), pp. 92 ff.

Chapter Eight

1. See the research studies of Dr. Diana Baumrind, which she describes in the following periodicals: "Parental Love and Parental Control," *Children* 12, no. 6 (Washington, D.C.: Childrens Bureau Administration for Children, Youth and Families, Office of Human Development Services Nov.-Dec. 1965): 230 ff; "Effects of Authoritative Parental Control on Child Behavior," *Child Development* 37, no. 3 (Chicago: University of Chicago Press for the Society for Research in Child Development, Sept. 1966): 87 ff; "Authoritarian vs. Authoritative Parental Control," *Adolescence* 3, no.11 (Rosyln Heights, NY: Libra Publishers Inc., Fall 1968): 255 ff.
2. See Dennis Guernsey, "What Kind of Parent Are You?" *Family Life Today*, January 1978, p. 4.
3. See Diana Baumrind, "Authoritarian vs. Authoritative Parental Control," p. 256.
4. See Dennis Guernsey, "What Kind of Parent Are You?" p. 6. Used by permission.
5. See Baumrind, "Authoritarian vs. Authoritative Parental Control," p. 260.
6. Ibid., p. 261.
7. See Dennis Guernsey, "What Kind of Parent Are You?" p. 6.
8. These statistics are part of "How Junior High Students See Themselves, Their Families, Their Friends," a fifty-question survey of 150 junior high students in public and parochial schools, plus church Sunday school classes, conducted by Jeff Ridenour as part of a course requirement in an independent study in sociology, Westmont College, Santa Barbara, California, 1982.

9. James Dobson, *The Strong-Willed Child* (Wheaton, IL: Tyndale House Publishers, 1978), p. 204. Used by permission.

Chapter Nine

1. Dr. James Dobson, *Preparing for Adolescence* (Santa Ana, CA: Vision House, 1978), p. 16.
2. See Thomas Gordon, *Parent Effectiveness Training* (New York: Peter H. Wyden, Inc., 1970), chapters 6 and 7; Robert Pedrick, *The Confident Parent* (Elgin, IL: David C. Cook Publishing Co., 1979), chapter 3; Haim Ginott, *Between Parent and Child* (New York: Avon Books, 1965), chapter 2.
3. See Thomas Gordon, *Parent Effectiveness Training*, pp. 148–264. Also, see comments on Gordon's philosophy in Appendix 2, "Resources for Parents."
4. Bruce Narramore, *Adolescence Is Not an Illness* (Old Tappan, NJ: Fleming H. Revell Co., 1980), p. 118. Used by permission.
5. Ibid., pp. 119, 120.
6. Psychologists and child training specialists differentiate between logical and natural consequences. Natural consequences happen "naturally" of their own accord. Logical consequences are set up ahead of time by the involved parties, according to what seems fair or "logical" to all concerned. For an informative discussion on natural consequences, see Bruce Narramore, *Help! I'm a Parent* (Grand Rapids: Zondervan Publishing House, 1972), chapters 5 and 6.

Chapter Ten

1. Actually, this is more a case of *natural* consequences, which happened of their own accord, rather than *logical* consequences, which are set up in advance. See chapter 9.
2. David Hartman and guest Barbara Levy, family counselor, "Good Morning, America!" American Broadcasting Company, broadcast May 12, 1982.

APPENDIX 1: TALKING ABOUT ATTITUDES

Following are conversation-starter questions which are also described in the conclusion. These questions are designed to help you establish communication with your teenagers regarding the basic attitudes that are discussed in this book. See page 179 of the conclusion for how to use or modify these questions for best results.

Letting Go

I want to work on deparenting, which means making you independent and responsible by the time you're ready for college or a job. Do you feel I give you enough freedom and independence for your age? Or, am I stifling you and making you feel like a little kid? If I am, what should I stop doing and what should I start doing?

Acceptance

Do I accept who you are as a person, or do you sometimes feel like I am stuffing you in the mold that I want for you? Do you have any interests or talents I'm not helping you develop? Do you feel like a special individual in our home? What can I do to make you feel special?

Thoughtfulness

Does what I say to you usually make you feel good or uncomfortable? Do my words build you up or tear you down? Is there any word or pet name that I sometimes use with you that bugs you? Do I ever say thoughtful things that encourage you? How can I encourage you more?

Perseverance (in listening)

Do you feel I listen to you when you talk? Or, am I sometimes too busy or preoccupied? Do you think I try to hear what you are feeling as well as saying? How could I listen to you better? Would you be willing to tell me when you don't think I'm listening?

Forgiveness

Do you think I get angry very often? Do you ever think I hide being angry? After I'm angry do I show forgiveness or do I sometimes seem to hold a grudge? What do I do that frustrates you or makes you angry?

Self-Control

Would you say I am consistent or inconsistent in discipline? When am I too strict? What do I say at those times? When am I too easy? How do I talk then? What would be a happy medium for you? Do you think I give you a chance to discuss things, or do I usually want it done my way, with no arguments?

Fairness

Do you think you are usually disciplined in a fair way? What am I doing that you sometimes think is unfair? How could we change this? Which do you prefer—a "you" message or an "I" message? (Explain both.) Would you like to use "I" messages sometimes to tell me how you feel? How would you like to try the Conflict Resolution Process? (Explain how it works.) Do you ever feel you win, at least a little bit, when we have a disagreement? Do you think logical consequences (explain) are fair? Is there a good way we can use them (or improve them if already using)?

Trust

Do you feel I trust you? Do you trust me? Are there some areas (friends, dating, etc.) where you don't feel completely trusted? How can we talk more about these areas and feel more relaxed about them? Do I ever act like I think you have to earn my trust? If so, what do I do or say?

APPENDIX 2: RESOURCES FOR PARENTS

BASIC PARENTING

How to Really Love Your Teenager, Ross Campbell, Victor Books, 1981. One of the best books you can read to help you understand and relate to your teenager. Strong chapters on communication techniques

Preparing for Adolescence, James Dobson, Vision House, 1978. Valuable help for parents of preteenagers and early teenagers (13–14). Can be read with your child. Strong on building self-esteem, confidence. Tape cassettes and a workbook are also available.

Parent Effectiveness Training, Thomas Gordon, Peter H. Wyden, Inc., 1970. Recommended with strong reservations, especially for parents dedicated to a total biblical view of parenting. Gordon's methods for communicating—active listening and the "I" message—are valuable tools for any parent to use. However, his views of authority (see especially chapter 10) will present problems for any biblically oriented parent. For a thorough review and critique of Gordon, see chapter 7 of *The Strong-Willed Child: Birth to Adolescence*, by Dr. James Dobson (Tyndale, 1978).

Building Positive Parent-Teen Relationships, Rex Johnson and Norman Wright, Harvest House, 1977. A total course of fourteen sessions that include "Identity and Self-Esteem," "How to Communicate as a Family," "Anger and Family Life," "Rules and Standards," "Dating and Sexual Behavior." Strong biblical emphasis, practical exercises, suggestions.

Parenting with Love and Limits, Bruce Narramore, Zondervan, 1979. Not a book on parenting teenagers per se, but one of the most useful books you can read to give a comprehensive biblical view of the task of parenting. A workbook for group study, *You Can Be a Better Parent*, is available.

BUILDING SELF-ESTEEM, CONFIDENCE

Hide or Seek, James Dobson, Revell, 1974. Many believe this to be Dobson's best book. Must reading for every parent.

You're Someone Special, Bruce Narramore, Zondervan, 1978. A comprehensive view of self-esteem from a biblical viewpoint. Can be especially helpful to those who have been confused by sermons or other input denouncing a desire for self-esteem as selfish or unchristian.

The Sensation of Being Somebody, Maurice Wagner, Zondervan, 1975. One of the best general discussions of self-esteem from a Christian viewpoint. A readable and useful tool for parents, or anyone seeking a better self-concept.

195

COMMUNICATION

Caring Enough To Hear, David Augsburger, Regal Books, 1982. See especially chapters 3 and 4 for insights into what communication is and how it works. Designed to help communication with those closest to you—spouse, children, friends.

See also: *Parent Effectiveness Training*, Thomas Gordon, described in Basic Parenting section above.

Communication: Key to Your Teens, Rex Johnson, Norman Wright, Harvest House Publishers, 1978. Similar in design and philosophy to Wright's classic book, *Communication: Key to Your Marriage*. Excellent chapter on "How to Trust Your Teenager."

The Family That Listens, H. Norman Wright, Victor Books, 1978. A concentrated and practical discussion of the entire area of communication with special emphasis on listening.

EMOTIONS

Feeling Free, Archibald Hart, Revell, 1979. Superb insights on how to control your emotions. Strong chapters on dealing with depression, anger, and guilt.

Blow Away the Black Clouds, Florence Littauer, Harvest House, 1979. Written in a conversational and compassionate style. Based on how the author dealt with tragedy and depression in her own life. Includes chapters on "How to Live with a Depressed Person," and "How to Counsel a Depressed Person."

Facing Anger, Norman Rohrer and Philip Sutherland, Augsburg Publishing House, 1981. Useful discussion of understanding anger, knowing the sources of anger and dealing with anger. See especially chapter 8, "How to Handle Anger in Others," and chapter 9, "How to Handle Anger in Yourself."

TEMPERAMENTS, PERSONALITY

Understanding the Male Temperament, Tim F. LaHaye, Revell, 1977. To help fathers understand themselves (and mothers understand fathers). Perhaps LaHaye's best treatment of the temperaments.

After Every Wedding Comes a Marriage, Florence Littauer, Harvest House Publishers, Eugene, Oregon, 1981. Helpful and down-to-earth advice for being a strong husband-wife team through an understanding of the four basic temperaments.

Personality Plus, Florence Littauer, Revell, 1982. How to amplify your strengths and overcome your weaknesses through a practical understanding of the four basic temperaments: Sanguine, Choleric, Melancholy, Phlegmatic. Based on the author's personal experience and seminar teaching over the past fifteen years. A gold mine of illustrations and examples of how one temperament relates to another, particularly in the family setting.

ABORTION

Abortion: The Silent Holocaust, John Powell, S. J., Argus Communications, 1981. A telling discussion of abortion that is rational, but not overemotional. The author does a skillful job of confronting the Christian with the value of a human being and the terrible tragedy in taking human life. A good book to share with anyone trying to decide where he or she stands on abortion.

FAMILY DEVOTIONS

Family Life Today Magazine, editor, Phyllis E. Alsdurf, Gospel Light Publications. Includes a monthly column, "Family Times Notebook," loaded with ideas for having family time and family devotions.

Family Fun and Togetherness, Wayne Rickerson, Victor Books, 1979. Practical ideas for making family night the best night of the week. Also ideas for what to do on vacations and how to celebrate special days and events. Dozens of ideas for games, hobbies, reading and planning good times for the family. A study guide also available.

Successful Family Devotions, Mary White, Nav Press, 1981. Developed by the author and her husband Jerry. Includes material on having devotions with young children as well as teenagers. Chapters on special occasions and special problems. The author wrote this book particularly for families who "can't sit still for formal devotions."

DRUG ABUSE

Drug Abuse: What Can We Do?, Lloyd V. Allen, Jr., Regal Books, 1981. A brief but helpful discussion of causes of drug use, with specific chapters on all types of drugs. Jay Kesler, president of Youth For Christ, has recommended this book for all staff members.

Drugs and Drinking: The All American Copout, Jay Strack, A Sceptre Book (Thomas Nelson), 1979. The author is an evangelist who writes out of four years of personal experience and suffering with drugs. His opening chapter, "Why Young People Turn to Drugs," is particularly helpful. Also has good chapters on recognizing symptoms of drug abuse and how to counsel the drug user. Includes glossary of terms.

ALCOHOL, ALCOHOLISM

I'll Quit Tomorrow, Vernon E. Johnson, Harper and Row, 1980. One of the best discussions available for helping families deal with an alcoholic member. Johnson is founder and president emeritus of the Johnson Institute, Minneapolis, Minnesota. He has traveled extensively and lectured widely on the effective treatment of alcoholism.

Sipping Saints, David Wilkerson, Spire Books, 1978. A strong argument against drinking in the author's hard-hitting, mince-no-words, style. Includes a list of Scripture passages on what the Bible says about alcohol. Especially thought-provoking chapters include " 'Responsible' Drinking," and "Be Honest, Sipping Saints!"

HOMOSEXUALITY

The Homosexual Crisis in the Mainline Church, Jerry Kirk, Thomas Nelson, 1978. A gentle but firm discussion of the problems of the homosexual. Kirk compassionately discusses how to minister to the gay person, and how to accept him as you realize his agony. The author speaks out against homosexuality but also condemns the "homophobia" which possesses many who are appalled by the practice. The author believes that there is hope for the homosexual to change with God's help.

Homosexuality: The Bond that Breaks, Don Williams, BIM, Inc., 1978. A lucid discussion of homosexuality and "gay theology." The author skillfully presents the teachings of Scripture and the homosexual interpretation of these passages. He has empathy for the homosexual as a person but shows how Scripture completely condemns the practice of homosexuality.

SUICIDE

Understanding Suicide, William L. Coleman, David C. Cook, 1979. Includes a helpful section on facing the tragedy of a suicide. Helps survivors grapple with questions like: "Was it my fault?" "Why did it happen?" Also includes chapters to help spot the potential suicide, what to do after an unsuccessful attempt. Includes a chapter on the youth epidemic of suicide.

Suicide: A Cry for Help, Helen Hosier, Harvest House Publishers, 1978. A good overview of suicide, its causes and resulting problems. Includes a good chapter on suicide among youth. The Appendix offers two sources of help for those dealing with suicide problems: (1) CONTACT—Teleministries, U.S.A. and (2) a Directory of Suicide Prevention Agencies in the United States.

DISCOURAGED AND DISTRESSED PARENTS

Parents in Pain, John White, Inter-Varsity Press, 1979. A helpful combination of practical suggestions for dealing with wayward teenagers and realistic and inspirational counsel for parents who feel guilty, frustrated, and angry because of serious problems with their son or daughter. A counsellor and a professor of psychiatry, White deals with a wide range of problems from lack of trust to alcoholism, homosexuality, and suicide.

Teenage Rebellion, Truman E. Dollar and Grace H. Ketterman, M.D., Fleming H. Revell, 1979. The authors represent over fifty years of experience in working with distressed young people. They explore the pressure and causes of teenage rebellion and what parents can do to relate to their children more effectively. Includes a strong chapter, "The Father—More Than a Biological Necessity."

Do You Know Where Your Children Are?, John Benton, Fleming H. Revell, 1982. Offered as a discussion of the runaway teenager or potential runaway, the book is loaded with excellent material for building a better relationship with your teenager. The author, along with his wife, operates the Walter Hoving Home in Garrison, New York, which specializes in helping delinquent and runaway girls. He also has children of his own and writes not only from long years of experience with troubled teenagers but with the empathy of a parent.

APPENDIX 3: TEMPERAMENT TEST SCORING

To score the Temperament Test, transfer your marks on pp. 74–75 to this sheet, add up your strengths and weaknesses, and combine both sets of totals to see which temperaments are the strongest.

STRENGTHS

	SANGUINE	CHOLERIC	MELANCHOLY	PHLEGMATIC
1	__ Animated	__ Adventurous	__ Analytical	__ Adaptable
2	__ Playful	__ Persuasive	__ Persistent	__ Peaceful
3	__ Sociable	__ Strong-willed	__ Self-Sacrificing	__ Submissive
4	__ Convincing	__ Competitive	__ Considerate	__ Controlled
5	__ Refreshing	__ Resourceful	__ Respectful	__ Reserved
6	__ Spirited	__ Self-Reliant	__ Sensitive	__ Satisfied
7	__ Promoter	__ Positive	__ Planner	__ Patient
8	__ Spontaneous	__ Sure	__ Scheduled	__ Shy
9	__ Optimistic	__ Outspoken	__ Orderly	__ Obliging
10	__ Funny	__ Forceful	__ Faithful	__ Friendly
11	__ Delightful	__ Daring	__ Detailed	__ Diplomatic
12	__ Cheerful	__ Confident	__ Cultured	__ Consistent
13	__ Inspiring	__ Independent	__ Idealistic	__ Inoffensive
14	__ Demonstrative	__ Decisive	__ Deep	__ Dry Humor
15	__ Mixes Easily	__ Mover	__ Musical	__ Mediator
16	__ Talker	__ Tenacious	__ Thoughtful	__ Tolerant
17	__ Lively	__ Leader	__ Loyal	__ Listener
18	__ Cute	__ Chief	__ Chartmaker	__ Contented
19	__ Popular	__ Productive	__ Perfectionist	__ Permissive
20	__ Bouncy	__ Bold	__ Behaved	__ Balanced
	TOTALS _____	_____	_____	_____

WEAKNESSES

	SANGUINE	CHOLERIC	MELANCHOLY	PHLEGMATIC
21	__ Brassy	__ Bossy	__ Bashful	__ Blank
22	__ Undisciplined	__ Unsympathetic	__ Unforgiving	__ Unenthusiastic
23	__ Repetitious	__ Resistant	__ Resentful	__ Reluctant
24	__ Forgetful	__ Frank	__ Fussy	__ Fearful
25	__ Interrupts	__ Impatient	__ Insecure	__ Indecisive
26	__ Unpredictable	__ Unaffectionate	__ Unpopular	__ Uninvolved
27	__ Haphazard	__ Headstrong	__ Hard-to-please	__ Hesitant
28	__ Permissive	__ Proud	__ Pessimistic	__ Plain
29	__ Angered Easily	__ Argumentative	__ Alienated	__ Aimless
30	__ Naive	__ Nervy	__ Negative Attitude	__ Nonchalant
31	__ Wants Credit	__ Workaholic	__ Withdrawn	__ Worrier
32	__ Talkative	__ Tactless	__ Too Sensitive	__ Timid
33	__ Disorganized	__ Domineering	__ Depressed	__ Doubtful
34	__ Inconsistent	__ Intolerant	__ Introvert	__ Indifferent
35	__ Messy	__ Manipulative	__ Moody	__ Mumbles
36	__ Show-Off	__ Stubborn	__ Skeptical	__ Slow
37	__ Loud	__ Lord-over-others	__ Loner	__ Lazy
38	__ Scatter-brained	__ Short tempered	__ Suspicious	__ Sluggish
39	__ Restless	__ Rash	__ Revengeful	__ Reluctant
40	__ Changeable	__ Crafty	__ Critical	__ Compromising
	TOTALS _____	_____	_____	_____
	COMBINED TOTALS _____	_____	_____	_____

Taken from the *After Every Wedding Comes a Marriage Workbook*, copyright 1981, Harvest House Publishers, Eugene, Oregon. Used by permission.

APPENDIX 4: ANSWERS TO PARENTING STYLE QUIZ (pp. 144–45)

1. Clearly authoritarian, and one of the most irritating remarks you can make to a teenager, according to the ones I surveyed.

2. This is an authoritative inquiry. A curfew was broken, but the parent is willing to hear the teenager's side.

3. Permissive, of course, and easy to do if you are feeling guilty about wanting to stay up and enjoy the game yourself.

4. This sounds like logical consequences, but it is really authoritarian. I used it with my sons, until I learned better.

5. It's easy to be permissive when you feel noble. Teenagers are masters at bringing out one's nobility.

6. Authoritarians often say, "Just do it."

7. The authoritative parent can admit he is wrong, but he doesn't back off on an important issue.

8. Authoritarians often say, "Enough of that."

9. This sounds like an authoritative parent doing a little active listening.

10. Well, yes, this is being permissive, but the alternative is (gasp) riding the school bus!

11. Authoritative parents are willing to give teenagers a chance to blow it (under reasonable conditions, of course).

12. Permissive parents are always there as a helpful resource. And, again, it makes them feel noble.

13. When anger flares the cooler authoritative head is more likely to prevail.

14. Authoritative parents understand, but also ask for what they need.

15. Permissiveness makes peace whenever it can. No price is too high.